OVERSOLD AND UNDERUSED
COMPUTERS IN THE CLASSROOM

OVERSOLD AND UNDERUSED

COMPUTERS IN THE CLASSROOM

Larry Cuban

HARVARD UNIVERSITY PRESS

Cambridge, Massachusetts   London, England   2001

Library of Congress Cataloging-in-Publication Data

Cuban, Larry.
Oversold and underused : computers in the classroom / Larry Cuban.
p.   cm.
Includes index.
ISBN 0-674-00602-X
1. Computer-assisted instruction—United States—History.
2. Educational technology—United States—Evaluation.   I. Title.

LB1028.5 .C77 2001
371.33′4—dc21   2001020420

CONTENTS

For Barbara
Who with patience and love
has taught one slow learner
the geography of the heart

INTRODUCTION: REFORMING SCHOOLS THROUGH TECHNOLOGY

School reform again, again, and again. If any aspect of schooling in the past two centuries has escaped the reformers' passion for improvement, I have not found it. From ineffective teaching to unhealthy lunches, from insufficient parental involvement to inadequate science curricula, from mixing grade levels in classrooms to building schools without walls—no aspect of schooling has evaded the reformers' scrutiny. Few people in these professions remain unemployed for long.[1]

Bashing schools and teachers is common fare in the rhetoric of reform. Advocates for change must mobilize supporters, and they do it by dramatically calling attention to school problems. Yet, paradoxically, like most Americans, the very same people who denigrate current education practices also profess an enduring faith in the power of schools to make a better society while placing individual students on an escalator toward financial success. Like most Americans, reformers believe that education is a solution for both individual failures and larger social problems. "Just see wherever we peer into the first tiny springs of the national life," Andrew Carnegie wrote in 1886, "how this true panacea for all the ills of the body politic bubbles forth—education, education, education."[2]

When public kindergartens were introduced in the late nineteenth century, reformers hailed them as an alternative to the harsh conditions that prevailed in urban schools, particularly in those that immigrant children attended. These parents often waited until their children were seven or older before enrolling them in school. But with no adult at home during the day, these children frequently found their way into the street, seeking odd jobs or begging. The age-graded school began in grade 1 and was unforgiving to young children, they claimed, who were taught in large groups and moved lockstep from one lesson to another regardless of how quickly or slowly they learned. Many young children failed. Reformers saw kindergartens for 5- and 6-year-olds as a way to save urban children from both the chaos of street life and the regimentation of public schools, while helping immigrant families learn the practical skills of becoming American.

The first generation of kindergarten teachers were public-spirited women trained in the formal methods of the German educator Friedrich Froebel. Equipped with instructional materials that Froebel had designed, these teachers spent a half-day with 5- and 7-year-olds in classrooms. There, lessons on personal cleanliness, nutritious foods, and good manners blended with drawing, learning the alphabet, and playing with blocks. After the children went home for lunch, kindergarten teachers visited families in their crowded homes and helped mothers with everything from preparing healthy meals to filling out citizenship papers. The first urban kindergarten teachers were de facto social workers.[3]

Within a half-century, the kindergarten had become a fixture in public elementary schools. But in becoming a part of the established system, kindergartens changed. No longer were teachers required to make home visits. They became state-credentialed professionals whose job was largely to ensure that children were prepared academically and socially for the first grade. Not surprisingly, this program set the stage for another generation of early childhood reformers, who criticized kindergartens for having become academic bootcamps. To this new wave of activists at the end of the twentieth century, the kindergartens, like so many other school reforms, had themselves become the problem rather than the solution.[4]

Who are these people continually agitating for school reform? In the late nineteenth century, those who fought regimented schooling and promoted kindergartens came from political elites and urban middle-class families. During the early days of the civil rights movement in the 1950s, those who opposed racial segregation in schools were poor and middle-class southern blacks and whites, joined with top federal officials. Today, diverse coalitions of concerned parents and activists, decrying the toxic conditions of urban schools, have banded together to lobby federal and state policymakers to send government checks—vouchers—to parents to spend on their children's education as they see fit. The voucher movement has comprised middle-class Catholic parents, Orthodox Jewish rabbis, wealthy Republicans, academics, corporate executives, and black activists in low-income urban communities. Charter school advocates, magnet school promoters, and homeschoolers also draw from an equally diverse population who want a different kind of schooling for children than many public schools currently offer. School reformers are, in a word, us.

Why, then, do so many of us turn to our public schools as,

paradoxically, both the source of and the solution for society's worst ills? The answer is that most Americans believe fervently in the power of education to change lives. Schools are not sectarian, like churches. They are not exclusive, like IBM or General Electric. As public agencies go, they are singularly visible. And they are universally available. Consequently, time and time again, countless other social ills, from urban poverty, crime, and drug abuse to wars and economic depression, have led reformers to the schoolhouse door.

The Progressive movement at the beginning of the twentieth century, the civil rights movement in the 1950s and 1960s, and the sustained drive since the 1970s toward U.S. supremacy in the global economy—to cite three obvious instances—have reverberated throughout American schools and universities.[5] And as these examples illustrate, most popular educational reforms begin with finger-pointing. In the early 1980s, when top public officials and corporate leaders worried that America was losing its economic primacy, wave after wave of unrelenting criticism washed over K–12 schools and higher education. In the pungent words of the 1983 report, *Nation at Risk*, by the National Commission on Excellence in Education: "Our once unchallenged preeminence in commerce, industry, science, and technological innovation is being overtaken by competitors throughout the world . . . The educational foundations of our society are presently being eroded by a rising tide of mediocrity that threatens our very future as a Nation and a people." Reform-minded public officials and corporate leaders faulted high schools for turning out low-performing graduates unprepared for a fast-changing automated workplace. "If only to keep and improve on the slim competitive edge we still retain in world markets, we must dedicate ourselves to the reform of

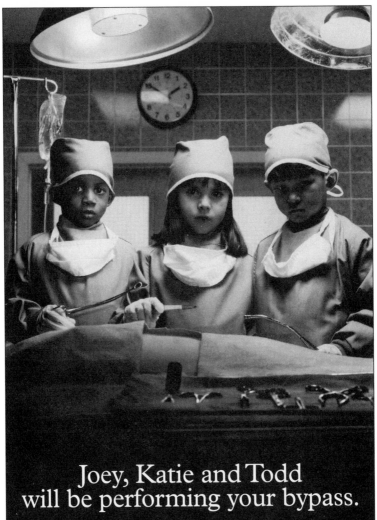

Joey, Katie and Todd will be performing your bypass.

Before you know it, these kids will be doctors, nurses and medical technicians, possibly yours.

They'll need an excellent grasp of laser technology, advanced computing and molecular genetics. Unfortunately, very few American children are being prepared to master such sophisticated subjects.

If we want children who can handle tomorrow's good jobs, more kids need to take more challenging academic courses.

To find out how you can help the effort to raise standards in America's schools, please call 1-800-96-PROMISE. If we make changes now, we can prevent a lot of pain later on.

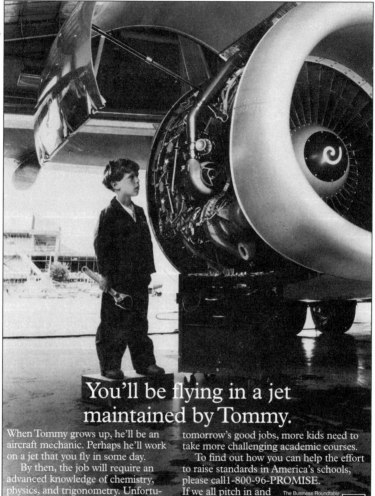

You'll be flying in a jet maintained by Tommy.

When Tommy grows up, he'll be an aircraft mechanic. Perhaps he'll work on a jet that you fly in some day.

By then, the job will require an advanced knowledge of chemistry, physics, and trigonometry. Unfortunately, very few kids are being prepared to master such sophisticated subjects.

If we want children who can handle tomorrow's good jobs, more kids need to take more challenging academic courses.

To find out how you can help the effort to raise standards in America's schools, please call 1-800-96-PROMISE. If we all pitch in and help, America will get where it needs to go.

our educational system for the benefit of all—old and young alike, affluent and poor, majority and minority. Learning is the indispensable investment required for success in the 'information age' we are entering."[6]

In the wake of the report, calls were heard from coast to coast for stiffer graduation requirements, tougher tests, greater teacher accountability, school restructuring, more advanced technology in classrooms, vouchers, better undergraduate education, and a general improvement in school efficiency. Yet neither the subsequent rise in test scores, the increase in numbers of students taking math and science courses, nor the economic boom of the 1990s silenced these doomsayers. The changes were inadequate.[7]

School activists in the 1990s, drawn largely from corporate, academic, and governmental elites—and endorsed, for the most part, by parents—concentrated on solving the nation's economic problems through education reform. They justified public school and university reforms as necessary to help the nation compete in a global economy and provide marketable information-age skills to future employees. Popular as it has been among parents and policymakers, this economic justification for schooling, coupled with faith in technical solutions for complex problems, has overwhelmed the civic and moral purposes for schooling children and youth that dominated throughout most of U.S. history.[8]

For almost two centuries, Americans expected that the public school—the *common* school, as it was initially called—would build citizens, promote equality, cultivate the moral and social development of individual students, and bind diverse groups into one nation. Nineteenth- and twentieth-century reformers understood that education—like anything else—has an economic side. The Massachusetts reformer Horace Mann, for example, had no difficulty in arguing for tax-supported public schools in the 1830s on grounds that graduates would bring to their employers literacy skills that would enhance their businesses. But Mann never argued, as current reformers do, that education is a servant of the economy. Nor did he ever urge schools to operate as businesses. Tax-supported public schools had a civic and moral mission that far exceeded the narrow economic aims of for-profit private corporations.

These earlier reformers assumed that tax-supported public schools were purveyors of common democratic values such as equality, fairness, toleration of differences, and justice. The inculcation of these values would ensure the survival of the Republic and the stability of the social order. Mid-nineteenth-century public schools and private colleges were expected to furnish the mind, strengthen moral character, and prepare citizens to discharge their civic responsibilities. Education was one and the same with the public good.

The end of the Civil War presented Abraham Lincoln's successors with an unprecedented opportunity to test these assumptions about education. In the conquered South, the monumental task was to transform four million ex-slaves into literate citizens. The federal government provided free public schooling for millions of black children and adults in the former Confederacy, thus forging new linkages between federal action and locally controlled schools. Race, citizenship, and equality came together for the first time in the public schools. This experiment in schooling ex-slaves for social democracy lasted only a decade, however. The issue of a federal role in schooling and educating poor, minority children was left unaddressed for another century.[9]

Social reforms in the early 1900s made explicit the proposition that public schools and higher education serve a fundamentally economic purpose. Businesslike efficiency and vocational education in secondary schools and colleges were seen as critical to preparing students for work in an industrial economy that was then competing with Great Britain and Germany. Meeting the soaring health and social needs of immigrant children also increased taxpayers' and parents' expectations of what their locally controlled schools and public-spirited new universities could do for the community and for each individual child. Public schools and universities were expected to Americanize newcomers and produce vocationally skilled graduates who could fill administrative posts and technically demanding manufacturing jobs in the ever-expanding industrial workforce. By the middle of the twentieth century, the social, civic, economic, and individualistic purposes of both public schooling and higher education were firmly in place. The growing conviction that a high school diploma was essential for each son and daughter to climb the socioeconomic ladder added to the fervor with which white, black, and foreign-born parents embraced the mission of public schools.[10]

During the Cold War, racial segregation and international economic competition came under the umbrella of problems that could be solved, in part, through education, extending beyond public high schools. For Americans, faith in universal schooling had become gospel. Schooling was a panacea for any disease at either the national or individual level.[11] But as the twentieth century drew to a close, poverty, social stratification, and racial inequities remained intractable. With increased immigration from Latin America and Asia and fierce scrambling for global market share, the purpose and performance of schools and universities again came under close scrutiny.

As this brief jaunt through U.S. educational history underscores, schools have served a number of broad social purposes in our democratic society. "You cannot have a democratic—indeed, civilized—community life," Neil Postman reminds us, "unless people have learned how to participate in a disciplined way as part of a group." The things children learn in school that matter in a democratic society were summed up cleverly by Robert Fulghum in his best-selling book *All I Really Need to Know I Learned in Kindergarten:* share what you have, play fair, don't hit, put things back where you found them, and clean up your own mess. David Labaree synthesized the social purposes that education serves into three goals that Americans seek from their tax-supported public schools: democratic equality, social efficiency, and social mobility. He argued that the goals of social efficiency (schools serving broad societal needs) and social mobility (individuals striving to be financially and socially successful) have merged to become the rationale for economic competitiveness—and in the last two decades have trumped democratic equality.[12] Now, as public schools and higher education are being asked to build the human capital that many believe is essential to sustaining technological innovation and global competitiveness, these other historic and broader civic purposes appear to be no more than distractions.[13]

Since the mid-1980s, private sector management has become the model for solving the problems of schools and universities. Educational activities are "downsized," "restructured," and "outsourced." School buses, lunchrooms, and stadiums carry advertisements for corporate sponsors. Logos of major corporations dot school corridors. In kindergartens, high schools, and universities, banner ads run across every computer screen wired to the Internet.[14] But perhaps more striking is the recent commodification of high school and college credentials. Employers buy high school diplomas and college degrees in the workplace, and for eighteen-year-olds a high school diploma has become as much an economic necessity as soda or gasoline. College graduates are even more attractive. Getting a bachelor's degree now seems to be within the grasp of any high school graduate willing to spend four years taking courses (on a campus or delivered on a home computer) and piling up debts. Students and employers alike now shop for schools and credentials as they would any other product sold in the marketplace.[15]

Critics of this wholesale embrace of market competition ask: Is everything educational for sale? Is being a good citizen about nothing more than being a good consumer? What about the "common good" the founders of public schools and universities so fervently sought to foster? In the first decade of the twenty-first century, these questions about public and private interests, tensions between the common good and individual preferences, have yet to be asked openly by candidates for public office, corporate leaders, school administrators, practitioners, and university presidents. Instead, what dominates media and policymakers' discussions of education is that schools achieve success on business-style assessments such as standardized test scores (de facto profit sheets) through business-inspired technical means.[16] And no tool is better suited for those economic ends than computers. Securing more and better computer technologies for schools, so that they can operate more efficiently and faster and support better teaching and learning, has been touted by corporate leaders and public officials as a splendid way to reform schools according to the market-driven agenda of the past two decades.

REFORMING SCHOOLS THROUGH
NEW TECHNOLOGY

Since the early 1980s, a loosely tied national coalition of public officials, corporate executives, vendors, policymakers, and parents have included in their reform agendas the common goal of creating more access to new technologies in schools. In this book, when I use the phrase "new technologies" I refer to the "hard" infrastructure of wiring, computers, software applications, and other equipment, including laserdisk players, overhead-mounted presentation machines operated from a keyboard, digital cameras, and so on. New technologies also include the "soft" infrastructure of technical support for all of this equipment, including scheduled replacement and professional development of teachers and administrators. When I refer to "old technologies" I mean textbooks, blackboards, overhead projectors, television, and videocassettes.

Some promoters within the coalition seek profit from selling equipment and software in the school market. Others seek a swift solution to thorny problems that historically have crippled education. Still others see an electronic revolution in classroom teaching practices. And some promoters, committed to social justice, want to ensure that poor and minority children will not be left behind in the rush for technological expertise. From many different directions, then, coalition advocates have pressed school boards and superintendents to wire classrooms and purchase new hardware and software, in the belief that if technology were introduced to the classroom, it would be used; and if it were used, it would transform schooling.[17]

Three different goals for high-tech hardware and software in schools unite this disparate but powerful ad hoc coalition:

- Goal 1: Make schools more efficient and productive than they currently are.

Behind the surge of automation in manufacturing, banks, insurance, and the new economy has been the impulse for efficiency—getting more work done at less cost. Although in the early days of computerization a debate raged among economists about whether the introduction of computers to the workplace was in fact increasing productivity, the economic prosperity of the 1990s, unrivaled in the twentieth century, has now convinced most doubters that information technologies have accelerated American workers' productivity. As a consequence, introducing electronic tools into schools has become a priority of corporate leaders and public officials.[18]

Louis Gerstner, Jr., IBM's Chief Executive Officer, minced few words about the task facing American schools: "Before we can get the education revolution rolling, we need to recognize that our public schools are low-tech institutions in a high-tech society. The same changes that have brought cataclysmic change to every facet of business can improve the way we teach students and teachers. And it can also improve the efficiency and effectiveness of how we run our schools."[19] Reformers such as Gerstner believe that computers can streamline administrative tasks, end wasteful paper flow, and enhance communications among professionals within and across organizations. Moreover, teachers in the classroom can use information technologies to convey far more knowledge and skills to students in less time. This dream is similar to that of reformers who introduced film, radio, and instructional television to schools in the 1950s, 60s, and 70s. The productivity gains, advocates then and now have claimed, can be captured in less money spent on administrative positions, faster and easier communication among professionals and between teachers and students, efficient teacher preparation for classes, better student grades on report cards, and higher standardized achievement test scores on international assessments. The goal has been "to make teachers more productive, not to replace them completely."[20]

- Goal 2: Transform teaching and learning into an engaging and active process connected to real life.

Many corporate leaders, academics, and practitioners believe that traditional forms of teaching (for example, reliance on textbooks, whole-class instruction, lecturing, and multiple-choice tests) are obsolete in the information age. "Students don't have to be tethered to a desk at all times," says America Online Chairman Steve Case. Critics often contrast traditional instruction with active classroom learning, in which teachers are closer to being coaches than drill instructors. They structure activities that give students choices while pressing them to learn subject matter in greater depth. These practices engage students in projects that cut across content boundaries and connect to learning outside the classroom. Sometimes called "student-centered teaching" or "constructivist practices," these forms of teaching, less evident in American classrooms, are, according to reformers in the coalition, essential for student learning in the twenty-first century.[21]

To constructivist-oriented reformers, computers offer ways of motivating students to learn about subjects they would seldom engage otherwise and to come to grips with real-world issues. Moreover, new technologies can create a deeper understanding of complex concepts by integrating different disciplines through work on individual and group projects. They can revolutionize classroom practice and prepare the next generation for an emerging workplace whose texture and boundaries few can predict with confidence.[22]

- Goal 3: Prepare the current generation of young people for the future workplace.

A driving force behind the effort to get more computers into schools is the changing job market. Susan Hammer, Mayor of San Jose, said: "Twenty-first century technology is everywhere: at gasoline pumps, supermarket checkout lines and our telephone answering machine. Everywhere, until recently, but in our schools. San Jose was woefully ill equipped to give students skills they need for jobs in our own backyard."[23] Reformers are convinced that most well-paying jobs in the future will require technological knowledge and skills and that students must be prepared for a far more demanding workplace than their parents faced.

At a 1996 national Educational Summit meeting held at the corporate headquarters of IBM, state governors, corporate leaders, federal officials, and a sprinkling of educators heard President Clinton address the group on the importance of academic standards, tests, and technology. The final official statement from the Summit wrapped the three divergent purposes holding together the ad hoc reform coalition into one sentence: "We are convinced that technology, if applied thoughtfully and well-integrated into a curriculum, can be utilized as a helpful tool to assist student learning, provide access to valuable information, and ensure a competitive edge for our workforce."[24]

The separate lobbying efforts of these very different groups within the ad hoc coalition during the economic expansion of the 1990s have been extraordinarily successful in generating federal, state, and local funds for building the necessary technological infrastructure within schools. In 1996 President Clinton made $2 billion available for five-year grants from the Technology Literacy Challenge Fund. In addition, the President laid out four "pillars" (or goals) which he challenged the nation to achieve.

1. Modern computers and learning devices will be accessible to every student.
2. Classrooms will be connected to one another and to the outside world.
3. Educational software will be an integral part of the curriculum—and as engaging as the best video game.
4. Teachers will be ready to use and teach with technology.[25]

Pillars 1 and 2 provide access to electronic equipment and networks; policymakers assume that after access is provided, Pillars 3 and 4 will follow as the night follows the day.

Both President Clinton and Vice President Gore also proposed (and Congress authorized) the "E-rate," a universal phone service subsidy that had been included in the previous deregulation of the telephone industry. The E-rate discounted the cost of wiring classrooms to the Internet in schools with high percentages of low-income students.[26]

Reformers have been astonishingly successful in wiring schools and equipping them with computer stations. Consider, for example, that in 1981 there were, on average, 125 students per computer in U.S. schools. A decade later, the ratio was 18 to 1. By 2000 it had dropped to 5 students per computer. But those are just ordinary computers. Multimedia computers, between 1997 and 1999, went from 21 students per machine to fewer than 10. And Internet-connected computers saw similar drops in the ratio of students to machines.[27]

These figures suggest only the barest outline of the major investments that have been pumped into the project of computerizing schools. In addition to start-up costs for hard infrastructure, there are soft infrastructure costs associated with technical support, scheduled replacement of obsolete equipment, and professional development. Altogether these monies add up to a multibillion-dollar investment. McKinsey and Company estimated that in 1995 approximately $3.3 billion was spent on hardware, software, networking, and related costs—approximately 1.3 percent of the average annual per-pupil expenditure, or $75 per student. By 1998–1999, spending had increased to $5.5 billion (excluding higher education), or $119 per child. These amounts are small by comparison to overall expenditure and to the levels of technology that experts have recommended. But compared to school district outlays a decade earlier, these amounts are substantial and increasing.[28]

Apart from federal, state, and local budgets, consider the private investment that families have made in providing home computers, electronic software, and Internet access for their school-age children. In a recent national survey, 60 percent of adults said that they have a computer at home, and almost one-third of this 60 percent have two or more personal computers. Among children ages 10 to 17 who said that they had computers at home, 88 percent told pollsters that they use them to do schoolwork.[29]

In seeking to achieve three divergent purposes, techno-promoters across the board assumed that increased availability in the classroom would lead to increased use. Increased use, they further assumed, would then lead to efficient teaching and better learning which, in turn, would yield able graduates who can compete in the workplace. These graduates would give American employers that critical edge necessary to stay ahead in the ever-changing global economy. In 2000 President Bill Clinton made the assumptions explicit: "Frankly, all the computers and software and Internet connections in the world won't do much good if young people don't understand that access to new technology means . . . access to the new economy."[30]

This interlocking chain of assumptions and beliefs dominates most policymaking about educational technology in the United States. One place to examine closely the accuracy of these assumptions would be where technological progress is most highly celebrated, where much has been invested to make new technologies available to teachers and students, and where great encouragement to use computers in classroom instruction is in evidence. Such a place is northern California's Silicon Valley. There, technology cheerleaders and resources are abundant, and schools offer a best case for exploring whether reformers' assumptions have materialized as predicted.

In examining the assumptions underlying the infusion of new technologies in Silicon Valley schools, I ask three questions.

1. In schools where computers are readily available, how do teachers and students use the machines in classrooms for instruction?
2. Have teaching and learning changed as a consequence of two decades of heavy promotion and investment in computers and other technologies? If so, what explains the changes? If not, what explains the stability?
3. Has the investment in computers and other technologies been worth the cost?

In Chapter 1 I describe the setting—the peninsula between San Francisco and San Jose in northern California, popularly known as Silicon Valley. This part of the state has made national headlines for having the highest average cost of a home, for the proliferation of dot.com billionaires, and for a frenzied pace of living. I explain why Silicon Valley, unique as it is, is an excellent place to study teacher and student access to computers, their use in schools, and the consequences—both anticipated and unanticipated.

Chapters 2 through 4 detail the actual use of computers by Silicon Valley teachers and students in early childhood education, high school, and university classrooms, along with the changes and stability in teaching that I observed. I chose early childhood programs and high schools because they represent entry and exit portals for the vast majority of students within public schools. I chose Stanford University in the heart of the Valley because it offered astounding access to information technologies in a noncompulsory setting very different from K–12 schools. The sharp contrasts of these three points in a student's career allow us to see the patterns—if any—that emerge.[31]

Chapter 5 offers three competing explanations for the anticipated and unanticipated outcomes that I observed in teachers' and students' use of new technologies. The final chapter responds directly to the question whether the investment in computers in classrooms has paid off, and it asks, further, whether the funds being spent to sustain new technologies bring American schools any closer to the broad civic and moral purposes that are at the heart of tax-supported public schooling.

1

THE SETTINGS

Silicon Valley was the source of changes taking place across society . . . The business of creating and foisting new technology upon others that goes on in Silicon Valley is near the core of the American experience. The United States obviously occupies a strange place in the world. It is the capital of innovation, of material prosperity, of a certain kind of energy, of certain kinds of freedom, and of transience . . . Silicon Valley is to the United States what the United States is to the rest of the world.

Michael Lewis, *The New New Thing*

In the national imagination and in historical fact, the state that gave the world Silicon Valley shimmers with contradiction. Today as in California's past, Gold Rush fever coexists with abject poverty; populist reforms vie with stark racism; fierce individualism masks a dependence on federal subsidies; Sierra splendor competes with Hollywood glitz. This amalgam of fantasies, desires, hard realities, and denials confounds even those who have lived their entire lives in the Golden State. The essayist and novelist Joan Didion, a native Californian, wrote of this "wearying enigma": "California has remained somehow impenetrable . . . We worry it, correct and revise it, try and fail to define our relationship to it and its relationship to the rest of the country."[1]

Referring to the latter, the journalist Peter Schrag wrote that although "it is nowhere written that any state or region has to play such a role, be such a symbol . . . without California, there is no national model, no place that, because of its unique history, geographic fortune, and cultural makeup, can combine promises of the good life with the social and economic affirmation that California once provided—and, just perhaps, could provide again."[2]

The territory of California entered U.S. history in February 1848 as the spoils of the Mexican War. Just one month earlier, on January 24, James Marshall had noticed a glint in the water rushing through his sawmill near the confluence of the American and Sacramento rivers. The discovery of gold touched off a rush of Europeans and Asians as well as fellow Americans into the region, seduced by the promise of instant riches. "All classes of our citizens," a New York *Herald* editorial observed in 1849, "seem to be under the influence of this extraordinary mania . . . Will it be the beginning of a new empire in the West, a revolution in the commercial highways of the world, a depopulation of the old States for the new republic on the shores of the Pacific?" At least the first two of these querulous predictions hit the mark.[3]

Continuous migration brought hundreds of thousands of newly minted Californians face-to-face with the terrible beauty of a land riven by mountains, faultlines, rivers, and deserts. As stunning as its natural beauty was, the land's fertility was equally remarkable, so long as water could be directed to the burgeoning fields and orchards. But how were entrepreneurs to transport their gold, silver, grain, fruit, and lumber to eager customers in the rest of the country? At the middle of the nineteenth century, the choices were an arduous four-week journey overland by wagon and boat to the east coast; or an ocean voyage from San Francisco to Panama, followed by a trek across the jungles of the Isthmus, and then another ocean voyage to New York—all of which could take even longer. With thousands of Irish and Chinese immigrants to do the backbreaking work and ample federal grants to support it, three San Francisco merchants set out to build railroad connections between the Midwest and the Pacific coast. When tracks from the east and west were finally joined in 1869, California metals, wheat, and oranges found ready markets across the nation, and a new era of transcontinental commerce was born.

Images as well as products flowed along those tracks, feeding a new, sometimes troubled, sense of national identity. In the *Octopus*, a 1901 novel about the sinister grip of the Southern Pacific Railroad on California, Frank Norris reflects on the main character Magnus Derrick, a wheat grower in the San Joaquin Valley: "It was the true California spirit that found expression through [Derrick], the spirit of the West, unwilling to occupy itself with details, refusing to wait, to be patient, to achieve by legitimate plodding; the miner's instinct of wealth acquired in a single night prevailed, in spite of all."[4] The California of America's imagination was a land of temptation as well as hope, where the recklessly ambitious could go from poverty to riches and back again in quick succession.

It was also a place where people could reinvent themselves. As early as 1868 the traveler John Muir, upon entering the state, had exclaimed in his diary: "Born again!"[5] Of course every prior frontier in the nation had presented opportunities to move, to be different, to experiment; but the lure of quick wealth in California gave both natives and immigrants added incentives to apply novel approaches to old problems. Kevin Starr, California State Librarian, said of this urge to start life anew: "The American people have turned to California for new models of lifestyle, new ways of enjoying and celebrating the gift of life, and California responded with an outpouring of architecture, landscaping, entertainment, sport and recreation, a new relationship to the outdoors—all of which expanded and enhanced leisure in these United States."[6]

If individuals could be transformed, so could institutions. When the English observer James Bryce commented in 1916 that Californians in the generations following the Gold Rush had "formed a society more mobile and unstable, less governed by fixed beliefs and principles" than other states, he was connecting the past to the political experimentation of the state after the election of Governor Hiram Johnson in 1910. In that era, a Progressive legislature amended the state constitution to allow for populist referendums, initiatives, and recalls, to force corporate monopolies such as the Southern Pacific Railroad to respond to the state's citizens.[7]

These paradoxical possibilities, deeply imprinted on the national imagination, have drawn generation after generation of young and old, of grade-school graduates and PhDs, of Iowans and Ohioans and, of course, Michoacans, San Salvadorans, Cantonese, and Saigonese as well to California's shores. And since the last quarter of the twentieth century, nowhere in California has the flashing beacon of fiction and fact, temptation and hope, blazed brighter than from the strip of land that is known around the globe as Silicon Valley.

THE VALLEY

The peninsula stretching from San Francisco to San Jose—home to thousands of computer and Internet companies—is acknowledged throughout the world as the epicenter of the ongoing electronic revolution. With over 1.5 million people in Santa Clara County alone—the heart of the Valley—one out of every six of them works in the multibillion-dollar microelectronics industry. Towns with names like Mountain View and Sunnyvale run together, confounding visitors; the fruit orchards that once gave the Valley its rural signature give way now to industrial parks and housing tracts.[8]

Along the Bayshore Freeway, the main link between San Francisco and San Jose, rush-hour traffic begins at 5:00 in the morning and 3:00 in the afternoon. Billboard after billboard, some renting for $100,000 a month, touts computer products. On that busy highway, workaholic engineers and programmers—proudly wearing T-shirts that say "Working 90 Hours a Week and Loving It"—drive Porsches, while first-generation immigrants steer oil-burning 8-cylinder Chevrolets to their production jobs. After work, those Porsches pull into garages on multimillion-dollar lots in Palo Alto, while the Chevrolets park on the streets of working-class neighborhoods in east San Jose, where a $750 per month one-bedroom apartment is considered dirt cheap.[9]

Despite the terrible traffic and the outrageous price of homes, to the engineers and programmers seeking start-up companies, venture capital, or profit-sharing plans that will make them overnight millionaires, the Valley is Paradise. What singles out this late twentieth-century electronic gold rush from its predecessor in the nineteenth century is not the craze for making money or the entrepreneurs' 24/7 workaholism but rather an unshakable faith in the capacity of technology to improve life.[10]

The wealth in Silicon Valley is stunning. If Santa Clara

of shopping requests. Someday he wants to be able to say: "That's mine—I wrote that—and it's sitting on a million desktops."[14]

Strahorn reflects the attitude of many who flock to Silicon Valley seeking their fortune in computers. Surveys in 1984 and 1999 asked respondents who worked 50 or more hours a week whether they agreed with the statement: "There's a gold rush mentality in this area with too much emphasis on making money." In 1984, 66 percent agreed; fifteen years later, 81 percent agreed. The 1999 survey found that 52 percent of the respondents worked more than 50 hours a week, compared with 19 percent of adults in Atlanta who worked such long hours.[15]

Current and aspiring millionaires find the boundaries between job and home fuzzy. Because so many of the companies are global, employees must be on call day and night, and communication devices make that intrusion possible. Being available twenty-four hours, seven days a week knocks down any walls that protect a private life from work. The *Mercury News* survey mentioned above asked if "job related stress and tension" affected the person's life off the job. In 1984, 38 percent of the respondents agreed; in 1999, 52 percent agreed. When asked to agree or disagree with the statement "I think I work too much," 65 percent of those polled who worked more than 50-plus hours agreed. And of the same group, 56 percent agreed that "my main satisfaction comes from my job."[16] "It's not so much a life lived," one anthropologist who studies workers and families in Silicon Valley said, "but a life managed." He reports that one mother approached raising her children as a crash project always in progress. She built up a computer database of child-development strategies to use with her children and shared the information with friends. Some parents interviewed expressed frustration that they can't work on their email and voicemail until after their children go to sleep.[17]

What drives this frenzy? Surely, simple greed motivates some people. For others, the motive is the fun of the chase, the tingle that accompanies risk-taking. Thirty percent of the high-tech employees polled by the *Mercury News* agreed with the statement: "I enjoy living in a place that's changing the world." One out of four information-technology workers agreed that "there's a thrill to working in this fast-paced place."[18]

Still another motive for the hurried pace is the strong belief that the project will make millions of people's lives better than they are now. An abiding faith in their contribution to technological progress, small as it may be, drives many. If any syllogism summarizes the deeply held beliefs that drive Silicon Valley venture capitalists, software engineers, and computer programmers, this may be it:

- Change makes a better society.
- Technology brings about change.
- Therefore, technology makes a better society.[19]

The ethos of wealth, workaholism, and faith in technological progress as an unalloyed good is not unique to the electronics industry in the Valley. These values are held as well by teachers such as Sofi Frankowski and construction workers such as Ed Bruno, who, like Chris Strahorn, share the highways and streets with yellow school buses and thousands of parents driving their preschoolers and teenagers to class. And it is in the Silicon Valley schools—part of California's state system of public education—that the historic values of the state and the contemporary ones of the Valley converge.

THE SCHOOLS

If one compares California's rank among the nation's public schools on various measures, both the prospects and problems quickly become evident. Despite over $40 billion in funding for 6,000,000 students, 270,000 teachers, 8,000 schools in just under 1,000 districts, California struggles to educate its students. Based on 1999–2000 statistics, this is how California ranks nationally:[20]

Number of students:	1st
Teacher salaries:	9th
Per capita personal income:	13th
High school graduation rate:	37th
Per pupil expenditures:	41st
Students per computer:	47th
Students per teacher:	50th

Most accounts of the successes and failures of California public schools pinpoint 1978 as the pivotal year when state voters approved Proposition 13. This law radically reduced taxes on property and therefore the monies for public schools, and moved funding authority from local school boards to the governor and legislature.[21]

In the 1950s and 1960s, California's schools were the envy of the nation. They offered staffing, services, and a progressive program that few places in the rest of the country could match: counselors, arts programs, school libraries, access to medical services, after-school programs, and other benefits. The Master Plan introduced in 1960 established a three-tiered system of higher education—two-year community colleges, four-year colleges, and state universities—that was virtually cost-free. Yet even during these flush times, most Mexican immigrants and blacks in California received inferior schooling.[22]

After 1978, according to most accounts, decline set in. In the early 1980s, the reduction in property tax revenues for schools coincided with an economic recession and a slow-down of federal spending in the defense industry, located largely in southern California. Meanwhile, immigration from Mexico, Southeast Asia, and elsewhere climbed sharply, increasing the numbers of children drawing on the limited resources of the public schools. Even as they frantically sought other streams of revenue, governors and legislatures cut spending on schools. Throughout the 1980s and early 1990s, administrators downsized staffs, upsized classes, allowed buildings to decay, and watched academic achievement slip away. Unrelenting blasts of criticism from corporate leaders, parents, and officials about the declining quality of education further reduced the public's confidence in its school system.[23]

One educational industry that did flourish during these decades was school reform. California schools have had a legacy of innovation stretching back to the late nineteenth century. When the Civil Rights movement in the 1960s uncovered major inequities in minority schooling, the state, still among the top ten in the nation in per pupil expenditures, went on a reform binge. There was scarcely a reform that California governors, legislators, and educators encountered that they didn't adopt. Eventually, however, the escalating value of property (and therefore the property tax hit on homeowners), combined with resistance to busing as a means of desegregating schools and rising concerns over the poor return residents were getting for each education dollar they paid, led to the first taxpayer revolt in the nation. Despite the fact that Proposition 13 passed overwhelmingly, forcing a commensurate cut in services and staff in California schools, school reforms just kept on coming.[24]

In 1982 Bill Honig campaigned for the post of state superintendent of education on a platform of returning to traditional schooling. Anticipating the *Nation at Risk* report, he pressed for rigorous academic courses, a coherent state curriculum, and more demands on students and teachers. His message resonated with corporate leaders, parents, and ultimately voters not once but three times. Elected in 1982 and re-elected in 1986 and 1990, Honig, with the heavy endorsement of the state's business community, launched a subject-centered reform movement, including more graduation requirements, new curricula, and state tests tied to the requirements and curricula. He was also instrumental in getting a fiscal floor for school funding into the state constitution (Proposition 98).[25]

Between Proposition 13 and Honig's reforms, California became a more tightly aligned system of state-funded schools that hewed closely to what any governor and legislature could agree on. That pattern has persisted into the twenty-first century even as the state's school population has become increasingly minority and as academic performance in the eight large urban areas has deteriorated even further.

In the midst of an economic revival in the mid-1990s that produced surplus funds for schools, Governors Pete Wilson and Gray Davis, although from different political parties, continued to innovate. They offered a disparate batch of reforms such as class-size reduction, standards-based curriculum, mandated state tests, probation for schools that perform poorly on these tests, and new technologies in schools.[26]

The dream of putting technologies into California classrooms that would revolutionize teaching and learning appealed to corporate leaders and public officials across the political spectrum. Here was a reform that both parties and the California Business Roundtable endorsed sufficiently to pry open the public purse. As State Superintendent of Schools Delaine Eastin put it in 1996: "Technology is an essential part of education as we approach the twenty-first century. Ninety percent of the jobs created from this moment on will require advanced technological training. To compete for these jobs, our children will have to be skilled in the use of information technology . . . If we allow our educational system to fall behind the tide of change in the larger world, we prepare kids for bit parts at best. As the marketplace changes, so do the skills that all students require. Today, the want ads for coal miners in Pennsylvania call for laptop computer skills."[27]

As economic prosperity has produced budget surpluses, California governors and legislatures have authorized ever-larger appropriations for schools to get wired, equip classrooms and labs with computers, install software, and train teachers to use the equipment. In 1997 Governor Wilson and the legislature appropriated over $100 million for the first year of Digital High School grants, equal to $300 per student, to install computer networks in each of the state's 840 high schools over the next four years. In addition, they authorized annual funding of $45 per student (to be matched by the district) for maintenance and upgrade of networks.[28]

Few California reforms have ever forged such a powerful if loosely connected coalition of public officials, corporate executives, parents, and educators who agreed on the task of getting teachers and students to use computers in schools. And nowhere is the voice of that coalition more nearly unanimous than in Silicon Valley.[29] The area's enormous wealth, demand for skilled workers, and passion for technological progress has created an abundance of computers and software for teachers and students. The ratio of numbers of students per computer in Silicon Valley schools—the standard by which access to new technology is commonly judged—far exceeds state and national figures. Yet that affluence occurs in a state where class size is still larger than in other states and where school systems are just beginning to overcome the losses in funding they sustained after Proposition 13.

My explicit assumption is that, to borrow Michael Lewis's phrase, the "new new thing" in school reform—computers—can be seen most clearly in Santa Clara County in the heart of Silicon Valley. Although high housing costs and concentrated wealth may be more evident in the Valley than elsewhere, these California schools and their encounters with technology resonate with thousands of school districts in the country seeking to emulate and exceed what is occurring in the Valley. Thus, where there is an abundance in technological wealth, one can examine closely the interlocking chain of reformers' assumptions: increasing access to computers in schools will lead to more classroom use which, in turn, will transform teaching and learning to produce the desired outcomes in graduates and the economy.

In the next three chapters, I examine Silicon Valley preschools and kindergartens, high schools, and universities where major efforts have been made to get students and teachers to use new technologies in their daily work. In concentrating on three different levels of formal schooling catering to toddlers, teenagers, and young adults, I detected definite patterns of classroom use in Silicon Valley schools. These patterns have prompted me to offer conclusions about expenditures for technology in schools and their overall worth not only in this small part of the state but throughout the entire country. My conclusions should give pause to policymakers, practitioners, and parents committed to investing more money in expanding access and use of new technologies.

2

CYBERTEACHING IN PRESCHOOLS AND KINDERGARTENS

The first-time visitor to the Benjamin co-op preschool, located in a less affluent part of a Bay Area city in the outer reaches of Silicon Valley, is struck by the spaciousness, color, and energy on display in the classrooms. Esperanza Rodrigues, a fourteen-year veteran of preschool teaching, the last eight at Benjamin, takes the visitor on a quick tour of her domain on a May morning. She presides over 30 mostly Latino 3- and 4-year-olds split between two classrooms, four aides, and a half-dozen parent-volunteers.[1]

Each room is large and filled with light, and the walls are decorated with students' artwork. There are learning centers for blocks, reading, play, and art. Cubbies for children's clothes, a bathroom and sink for washing hands, a small kitchen for preparing food, and piles of toys and books fill the ample space. Labels in Spanish identify objects in the room. Two Power Macs (5400/180) and a printer on an easily accessible table sit in one room and two older machines sit in the other room. The four computers look well-used.[2]

Rodrigues's gusto for her work and children spills into the classroom. She leans over to ask one 4-year-old what she is doing with the clay, touches a boy in the finger-painting corner to reassure him about his work-in-progress, and quietly communicates with aides and parent-volunteers. She asks one aide to take Angela to a table to work on letters of the alphabet; she points a parent to a tug-of-war between two boys over a toy. The parent intervenes. A 3-year-old girl comes over to Rodrigues, crying for comfort. She listens to what the child says between sobs and then whispers something in her ear that brings a smile; the child skips off to tell her friend what happened. Rodrigues frequently switches between English and Spanish as she swirls through the rooms, watching, listening, and encouraging each individual.[3]

Except during circle-time. Sitting in a half-circle on a brightly colored rug, 15 rapt preschoolers face Rodrigues, who sits on a low chair next to a computer. She leads them in a song "How Are You?" sung to the tune of "Frère Jacques." Afterwards, she holds up for the class, one at a time, large cut-outs of a triangle, square, circle, and rectangle.

For each shape, Rodrigues asks the whole group what it is. Individual children yell out in Spanish and English whether it is a triangle or circle. She offers a "Muy bien!" followed by a warm "Good, Miguel." She then gives the cutout to each child to touch and pass on to a neighbor.

Now Rodrigues turns to the computer monitor, where the same four shapes are displayed. She moves the cursor to each shape and then asks the class what each shape is. Again, a chorus of vigorous shouts in two languages fills the room, followed by bilingual compliments on the correct answers. Rodrigues then passes out to each child envelopes filled with smaller versions of the four shapes. Calling the children's attention to the cursor on the screen, she clicks on a rectangle on the screen and asks the class to pull that shape out of the envelope. She does the same with a triangle and the other shapes until all of the figures in the envelope are arrayed in front of each child. She then reviews with the class what each shape is, asking the children to repeat it in both Spanish and English. She ends the lesson with a reminder that the computers have "Millie's Math House" and other programs they can use to learn more about these shapes. This circle-time lesson on shapes lasts 15 minutes.

Later in the morning, when children choose which centers they want to work in, visitors watch them clustered around two machines looking at "Millie's Math House." Two 4-year-olds, Lucinda and Maria, are whispering to each other. Maria points and Lucinda hits the keys when the computer voice asks aloud what size shoes are pictured: big, medium, small? The computers are left on all day, and they are in constant use by one or two preschoolers. "Stickybear's Early Learning Activities" and other multimedia software delight the children with animation and clever graphics. One piece of interactive software runs English, Spanish, and Japanese language programs that ask students to repeat aloud words on the screen which have just been said. The children bring up these programs to the screen again and again, relishing the repetition. The children know how to access programs and use the mouse to click on icons. With an occasional interruption by an aide or Rodrigues, they largely work by themselves, teaching and learning from one another about what is happening on the screen.

Visitors coming away from Esperanza Rodrigues's classrooms would be impressed with the spell that this talented teacher and her aides weave over 30 very active preschoolers for an entire morning. Of course, Rodrigues would be the first to point out "loner" children who have yet to acquire important social skills and the emotional control necessary for making a satisfactory adjustment to kindergarten. She could also easily point to the lack of certain materials, the need for more computers and accessories, and numerous logistical problems that crop up daily.

Having heard about all of these issues, the visitors would still marvel at the self-direction and confidence that so many of the children display as they choose various learning centers and participate in circle-time lessons. They would admire how the children treat one another with both respect and affection—civic virtues that these 4-year-olds have mastered. And if the visitors are very observant, they might well note the singular way that this preschool teacher has integrated the use of the computer and software effortlessly into a lesson on a math concept.

For many parents and educators unfamiliar with Rodrigues's talents, computers for tykes is both exciting and distressing. Since the early 1980s, photos of diaper-clad babies facing computer screens and using a mouse have appeared in popular media and delighted (or alarmed) many Americans. The rapt engagement of the very young with software—one company even puts out CD-ROMs for 9-month-old infants—reminds adults not only that the electronic millennium is upon us but that very young children are virtual learning machines. It also raises a serious question that is seldom asked by parents, educators, and public officials who encourage such investments: Just because children *can* do something when they are young, *should* they do it?[4]

THE HURRIED CHILD

Parents are eager to get their children into Esperanza Rodrigues's classroom. But enthusiasm for early childhood education has waxed and waned over the last two centuries. At the beginning of the nineteenth century, parents were not so eager to send very young children to school. By the 1820s, however, "infant schools"—an innovation initially imported by American school reformers from Britain for pauper and orphan children—had become fashionable places for working-class and middle-class parents to send their 3- and 4-year-olds. Facing the demands of rapid industrialization, many parents had come to believe that little children could be taught and that early experiences in infant schools would help them become better prepared for the 3Rs in regular school. By 1840 almost 40 percent of all 3-year-olds in Massachusetts attended these early nursery schools.

Within a decade, however, the experts on child-rearing asserted that such early exposure to written language and numbers would fail to accelerate children's intellectual development: even worse, infant schools would stunt their growth, they claimed. The proper place for a young child was at home with Mother. By the late 1840s, infant schools had disappeared and been largely forgotten, save by historians who have documented this deep-seated ambivalence toward schooling young children.[5]

The kindergarten, an innovation imported to the United States from Prussia in the 1850s by followers of Friedrich Froebel (the designer of the original "children's garden"), began as private schools for middle- and upper-class families. They slowly spread across an industrializing nation and in the 1870s appeared in public schools. But it was not until the 1940s that substantial numbers of middle-class families begin to send their children voluntarily to public kindergartens.[6]

During the Great Depression the federal government subsidized childcare and nursery schools as a way to put unemployed teachers to work. As World War II got under way, public officials urged mothers employed in wartime jobs to send their children to these federally funded schools. But by the 1950s, the issue arose again whether a mother's proper role was rearing children rather than working outside the home, and questions were raised about whether nursery schools and kindergartens undermined the family and were worthwhile for young children.[7]

By the early 1960s, however, scientific evidence and the experiences of earlier generations of parents had accumulated sufficiently to convince more middle- and upper-class families that their sons and daughters would benefit sufficiently from early schooling to offset any possible damage to the family unit. J. McVicker Hunt, for example, drew from the work of ethnologists and social scientists to emphasize the critical importance of early experiences for the development of the young. Another psychologist, Benjamin Bloom, argued that IQ was virtually fixed by the age of 5—implying that any meaningful intervention in the development of intelligence must occur before that age. Still, as recently as 1970, only 20 percent of 3- and 4-year-olds attended public and private nursery schools.[8]

The late 1960s turned out to be watershed years for early childhood education. The work of the Swiss psychologist Jean Piaget earlier in the century on the stages of a child's growth became more broadly accepted among educators and parents. The phrase "developmentally appropriate" entered educators' vocabulary.[9] Piaget, who has had much influence in America on popular thinking about the stages of intellectual development in children, complained that Americans often asked him the same question: "How can children be accelerated through your stages of cognitive development?" He called it the "American question."[10] Speeding up academic work for small children, stemming from parental concerns over an uncertain economic future, helped make preschools more like kindergartens and kindergartens increasingly similar to first grade.

Around this same time, as scores of scientists and educators became involved in the Civil Rights movement and federally funded efforts to help largely low-income families in urban and rural settings, a smorgasbord of interventionist programs emerged. New findings on brain development underscored the importance of having a stimulating environment in the home during the early years and of identifying medical and social problems as early as possible. Among the school-based programs, the most famous became known as Head Start, a federal program for preschoolers from poor families. Under its banner, policymakers teamed with academics to try a medley of school-based interventions. Some innovative programs had scripts for teachers to follow in telling students what to do, when, and under what circumstances. These emphasized whole-group instruction in reading and math, limited choices for children, and clear boundaries of what were acceptable and unacceptable behaviors. Other programs pursued the nursery school model of educating the whole child and avoiding undue emphasis on academics. Sensitive to the different stages of intellectual, emotional, and social development, teachers in these programs would listen to children, engage in discussions with them, and ask them to choose art corners, a sand table, a storybook center, or blocks during the day. Other programs were hybrids of the two approaches.[11]

Head Start had become the poster child program for President Lyndon B. Johnson's War on Poverty. Although comprehensive evaluations of Head Start in its first decade had shown limited academic gains for former Head Start students in elementary school, strong social gains were eventually detectable in the form of fewer teenage pregnancies, fewer dropouts, and less delinquency during and after secondary school. Preschools for poor children became a rallying cry in both political parties.[12]

By the 1980s, as an expanding labor market and the rising cost of living brought more women—including single mothers—into the workplace, issues of child care, nursery schools, and early education came to the fore with an intensity that surprised even public officials. Increased pressure from parents and policymakers on preschool and kindergarten teachers to prepare their children academically for the first grade created much conflict among educators. Administrators purchased tests that would determine whether 6-year-olds completing kindergarten were ready for the first grade. The numbers of children who essentially "flunked" kindergarten because they were either academically or socially unready for first grade (and perhaps had failed one of these readiness tests) increased. Even with these concerns about hurried academic development among early childhood educators, preschools flourished.[13]

By 1999, 46 percent of 3-year-olds and 70 percent of 4-year-olds were in preschool. In 1970, by contrast, just over 20 percent of children in these age groups had attended private and public preschools. In 1999, 80 out of 100 families with children in preschool earned over $75,000 a year; 11 out of 100 earned between $10,000 and $75,000; and 9 families earned less than

$10,000. Head Start, which was established for the latter group, spent $4.7 billion in 1998 on children enrolled from families at or below the federal poverty line, but even that amount reached only 27 percent of eligible 3-year-olds and 48 percent of eligible 4-year-olds. By 2000, more than 40 states offered free or subsidized preschool.[14]

Back in 1989, when President George Bush convened all of the state governors to establish national goals, few officials were surprised that the very first goal was to have all children "ready" for school. Another goal was to have U.S. students first in science and math in the world—national recognition that global economic competition required rigorous academic schooling even if it began at age 3.[15] One parent who became annoyed with this pressure has described how her 5-year-old rushed to finish her week's packet of kindergarten homework at 7:45 A.M. "Eight pages plus three drawings to illustrate three books that we had read since Monday," Sharon Noguchi writes. "Welcome to Y2 Kindergarten. Jumpstart that math and reading. Sit down, be quiet and do phonics, counting, addition, patterns, and probability."[16]

Notwithstanding the mixed results of $21 billion spent on 12 million preschoolers over 30 years, Bush's affirmation of Head Start and preschooling largely meant that a national consensus had formed which overwhelmed those few critics who opposed sending 3- and 4-year-olds to preschool. Regardless of social class, most American parents now believe that the first year of life—between birth and baby talk—is critical to a child's later success as an adult. By the 1990s, child development experts were certain that the earlier children could be stretched intellectually, the better for their academic success later in life. "The allure of infant determinism," in Jerome Kagan's aptly skeptical phrase, had become firmly entrenched in American culture. Astute entrepreneurs were building for-profit preschool empires to gain financially from parents' faith that the first few years determine the trajectory of a child's life as assuredly as gravity determines that a apple will hit the ground when it drops from the tree. By the year 2000, the question of whether toddlers should be in school had largely been answered with a resounding yes.[17]

WHAT MAKES A PRESCHOOL "GOOD"?

For those early childhood programs anchored in the belief that growth of the whole child proceeds through a series of developmental stages, a "good" preschool or kindergarten would include the following:[18]

- a certified teacher who endorses a view of carefully nurturing each developing child;
- a daily program with a few structures organizing the available space and time to provide many choices for children growing at different paces (blocks, art, language, sand table, water table, dress-up, reading corner, and so on);
- materials that encourage imaginative play.

Examples of such programs would be the traditional American nursery school of the 1950s, British infant schools of the 1960s, and the Bank Street College (New York City) approach to early childhood education.[19]

Another version of a "good" preschool and kindergarten favors the intellectual development of the child and academic preparation for first grade. Such a "good" preschool or kindergarten would include the following:

- a certified teacher committed to preparing the child academically for the next level;
- a daily program in which the teacher structures the available space and time to provide a mix of direct instruction, small group tasks, and individual work focused upon the skills of reading, math, writing, and thinking;
- ample materials to carefully guide children in becoming skilled in each of the areas above;
- play activities during a small portion of the day, but no play at other times; work and play are separate activities.

Examples of such programs over the last quarter century would be the Abecedarian project in North Carolina, the Englemann-Bereiter preschool in Illinois the early 1960s, and other schools with tightly scripted procedures and materials for teacher and children to follow.[20]

Buried within each version of a "good" preschool and kindergarten is an implicit goal. From a developmental perspective, the goal is to see that the personal well-being of each child flourishes. From an intellectual perspective, the goal is to prepare the child for a successful school career that will lead to a high-paying job where skilled graduates contribute the human capital essential for a prosperous economy. Hybrid schools seek to reconcile or blend these two competing versions of "goodness."

Of course, computers can be justified and used in any of these variations of a "good" preschool or kindergarten. Esperanza Rodrigues's preschool is a hybrid which leans slightly toward the developmental view, although her classroom also contains tasks and materials that will equip her charges academically for kindergarten. She lets her preschoolers go to the computer centers in the two rooms at any time of the day and integrates the technology into a math lesson during circle-time. At George Elementary School in northern California, kindergarten teacher Mark Hunter also embraces an academic perspective that contains elements of the developmental point of view. One April morning in Hunter's classroom went like this:

After the twenty children completed their period at the five centers, Hunter, sitting on a tiny chair in front of the computer, calls them to sit on the rug in a half-circle around him. At the remote control, he clicks the keys to bring up on the 35-inch screen an alphabet game that the 5-year-olds know well. For the letters N, O, and P as they appear on the screen with animated figures and catchy tunes, the children stand, bend, and reach in well-rehearsed moves as they sing along with the animated figures. The children clap enthusiastically after they act out Z and then prepare to leave the room for recess.

Hunter is convinced that the children's daily use of the room's five computers to play games, use reading software ("Reader Rabbit," "Curious George"), and write a daily message that he prints out has accelerated 18 of his 20 students to become beginning readers. He knows that the other two will make their breakthrough soon.

Each morning, the children choose which center they will spend the next 45 minutes in. The choices include drill and practice on letters and numbers, using math manipulatives, writing a daily message, listening to stories, and working with computers. The rules for use of each center are printed in block letters. At the teacher's direction, the children dutifully move from activity to activity. After a period of whole-group instruction and recess, they again choose a center they wish to go to for the period. Every child, however, has to complete a daily message on the computer and show it to Hunter.

After he arrives in the morning, Hunter sets up the programs that he wants the children to use during the day. He does not allow the children to fiddle with booting up, finding the right program on the desktop screen, or shutting the computer down.

A seven-year veteran of elementary school teaching in two districts, Hunter is a former physical education teacher. Because he has two older brothers who are deaf, he first learned computers through the technologies that were available for the deaf. He also knows sign language. From this unique background Hunter came to believe that much can be learned kinesthetically, and he encourages children to move about, act out stories, and connect physical games to academics. He has worked with computers for many years and has received instruction through the federally funded technology project in his district, the one that also supplied two of the five computers in his classroom, as well as the 35-inch monitor.

During center time, four boys work diligently at two computers ("We are not allowed to have three at a computer. Mr. Hunter says so," Adam tells us). They are working on their daily message. David speaks the words aloud as he slowly hits the keys: "I" then "like" then "my" and finally "dog," (he ends his sentence with a comma). Adam comes over, as does Brian, to see what David has typed. The three boys have an exchange about whether you can end a sentence with a comma. They agree that it should be a period. Saying aloud "comma" repeatedly, Adam returns to his station, where Steven has been typing his message: "I am crase" [sic].

Teachers like Rodrigues and Hunter, who use computers frequently, manage to integrate the technology seamlessly into their daily routines. In our study of 11 preschool and kindergarten teachers in sites scattered throughout Silicon Valley and the San Francisco Bay area, however, teachers with this level of pedagogical skill with computers were exceptions. Although all teachers in the study had access to computers in school and most had them in their homes, they used computers in classrooms in far more limited and much less integrated ways than the two teachers just described, as we will see.

SILICON VALLEY PRESCHOOLS
AND KINDERGARTENS

We chose six preschool and five kindergarten classrooms in seven Bay Area sites on the basis of whether they had computers in their rooms, included families from a range of socioeconomic backgrounds, and were willing to let us interview teachers and students and observe the technologies being used (see Table 1).

Two questions guided our inquiry:

- How often and in what ways were teachers and children using computers in preschools and kindergartens?
- Given the availability of computers, in what ways have approaches to teaching and learning remained stable and in what ways have they changed?

The first question examines the common assumption that computer availability leads to increased teacher's and children's use of machines. Our second question examines whether in-

Table 1. Study Sites

School	Level	Social class	Teacher/ aides	No. of students	No. of computers
Head Start/A	Preschool	Low-income	Guerroa/2	18	1
Head Start/B	Preschool	Low-income	Ibana/3	18	1
Jefferson	Preschool	Low-income	Franklin/2	26	2
Benjamin	Preschool	Low-income	Rodrigues/4–6	30[1]	4
Baldwin/A	Preschool	Middle-to-upper	Allen/2–3	30	1
Baldwin/B	Preschool	Middle-to-upper	Michael/3	30	1
George	Kindergarten	Low-to-middle	Hunter	20	5
Martes	Kindergarten	Upper-income	Fisher	18	0[2]
Robles/A	Kindergarten	Middle-income	Roberts	20	4
Robles/B	Kindergarten	Middle-income	Russell	20	4
Bell	Kindergarten	Low-income	Ramirez	20	3

[1] The Jefferson and Benjamin classrooms were at one site with two large rooms. The teacher, parents, and aides moved between the two rooms during the day; the Baldwin site had 30 children—15 in the morning and 15 in the afternoon.

[2] School policy provided in-class computers from grade 1 upwards. Kindergarten students went to the school's computer lab once a week for 30 minutes.

creases in classroom use would then lead to the transformation of teaching and learning.[21]

Student Use of Technologies at Sites

How frequently and in what ways did students use computers in these preschools and kindergartens? The most frequent use of computers occurred during "choice time." At ten of the eleven sites children were given the opportunity for 30 to 60 minutes a day to choose among centers structured for painting, playing with blocks, reading, and other activities, including computers.[22] Children were neither obliged to go to the computer center nor expected to produce a product, except for the "daily message" in Hunter's room.

Access to the computer center was typically first-come-first-served, with children regulating turns in various ways: asking the teacher, having a timer at the center, or negotiating turns among themselves. When many children wanted to use the machines, some teachers had a sign-up sheet. Because of the limited time in centers, not every child was guaranteed a turn at a computer, except at two sites (Benjamin and Baldwin A preschools), where the computer centers were available all day or when teachers rotated students through the computer center.

In three sites where center time was used (Jefferson, George, and Bell), teachers assigned children to use the computers for 30 to 60 minutes at least once a week. In this way, all children at these sites had access to computers. For the 70 children in these sites, this amounted to 10 to 15 percent of the time that they were in school. At two sites (Martes and Bell), where there were school computer labs and the entire class went for another 30 to 60 minutes once a week, each child had a personal computer available.

Overall, of the 250 preschoolers and kindergartners in these eleven classrooms, computers were available to at least 180 children curious or eager to work on computers for very brief periods of time (from 1 to 6 percent of the weekly time they were in school). If there were boys and girls among the 180 who skipped the computer center because they were fearful of the machines or were more interested in other centers, we classified them as "nonusers" of the technology.

For the most part, teachers loaded software that was appropriate to the children's ages, and the students' choices were limited to the software that the adults had selected. Two of the eleven teachers permitted children to insert CD-ROMS of their choice. The rest did not. Only two teachers permitted the students to print out what they had done on the computer.

Robles kindergarten teacher Paula Rosen typifies the majority of early childhood teachers who used computers regularly. There were four Macs in her room, two of which did not work. She had two others stored in a closet. Paula lets the students use the two that are working every day during choice time right after lunch. She calls the software such as "Jump Start," "Math Rabbit," "Franklin Learns Math" that she has loaded on the machines "games."

Paula promotes computer use 30 minutes a day because she believes that the software motivates 5-year-olds and is already ubiquitous in their homes. Although Paula believes the applications—some of which are drills—extend concepts the children already have learned in class, she does not require every student to go to the computers. Paula uses computers solely for enrichment and reinforcement, rather than direct instruction. District-provided training has equipped her with sufficient skills to manage these software applications and to do minimal troubleshooting of hardware problems.

During choice time, five students cluster around one computer running "Franklin Learns Math," a popular game with the kindergartners. Two sit on chairs while the others stand behind them. There is a timer that the 5-year-olds use only when one of their classmates stays too long. On occasion, a fidgety kindergartner will turn the dial to speed up the timer.

Much collaboration occurs among the children clustered around the computer. They provide answers to "Franklin" prompts. When the timer goes off (without any prior fiddling), each child calmly moves over and lets the next one take a turn. All of the children we observed had a quiet, confident expertise with the programs and computer. All of those we interviewed had computers at home.

Of the eleven teachers, five (including Esperanza Rodrigues at the Benjamin and Mark Hunter at the George) found explicit ways to blend the technology in their rooms into their instructional repertoire and to fit computers to what children were expected to learn. Two teachers (Rodrigues and Sherry Franklin at Jefferson) also created instructional materials for the computer and used them with the children, usually when they convened the entire group for particular lessons. Hunter used commercial software with the lyrics of a song and eye-catching animation to explain points on a 35-inch monitor and to bring the class to order to sing together. In her all-day kindergarten class, Felicia Ramirez (at the Bell school) tied together the day's lesson on firefighters to instructions at the computer center to use the art program to draw a firefighter, print it out, and give it to the firefighter visiting that afternoon. Marvin Michael (at Baldwin B) taught students who came to the computer center how to match letters with the keys on the keyboard and to type a title for an art project.

Table 2 summarizes the frequency and uses of computers and the level of integration of technology into classroom curriculum and instruction for the eleven teachers. The initial level is entry (first months of using computers). Then adoption (teachers generally use text, lecture, and conventional approaches but introduce lessons to teach students how to use keyboard, mouse, and elementary applications). After adoption, the next level of integration is adaptation, when most of classroom time is still spent in conventional ways of teaching but students spend about one fourth or more of their time using computers for homework and daily work in class. The next level is appropriation, where the teacher is fully confident in the use of computers and integrates technology regularly into daily routines. The highest level is invention, where teachers experiment with new ways of networking students and colleagues and use project-based instruction and interdisciplinary approaches.[23]

Students' Experiences with Technology at Home and School

From observations and interviews, it was clear to us that having a computer at home added considerably to the child's competence and confidence in booting up the computer and navigating software with a mouse. Of the 26 students (14 girls, 12 boys) across the seven sites that we observed and interviewed, 20 (10 girls, 10 boys) had computers at home and five did not (because of language difficulties, one child did not answer). Of the six children in Head Start, three had computers at home. All of the Martes children, according to the kindergarten teacher, had computers at home.

To the question of who taught them to use the computer, children's answers varied widely. Four children proudly told us that they taught themselves. The rest cited their father, mother, older sister, brother, or a mix of these. At home, the children reported using computers to play games such as "Nuclear Strike" and "Blue's Clues" and to use educational software ranging from "Reader Rabbit" to "Grandma and Me" to "Jumpstart Math." When we asked about other home technologies that the children used regularly, we found that 13 of the 26 could use a radio, 12 could manage the VCR, and 12 said that they knew how to use a CD player. Eight told us that they could use a microwave. Most of the children from families spanning the socioeconomic spectrum had broad exposure to electronic appliances in their homes, including computers; we noted no

Table 2. Frequency, Deployment, and Integration of Computers

School	Level	Frequency of use	How computers are deployed	Level of integration[1]
Head Start/A	Preschool	60 minutes a day	Centers/ free choice	Adoption
Head Start/B	Preschool	60 minutes a day	Centers/ free choice	Adoption
Jefferson	Preschool	90 minutes; each child assigned to center once a week	Centers/ free choice; required once a week	Adaptation
Benjamin	Preschool	Available all day	Centers/ free choice	Adaptation
Baldwin/A	Preschool	Available all day	Centers/ free choice	Adoption
Baldwin/B	Preschool	At teacher's discretion	Centers/ free choice and teacher's discretion	Adoption
George	Kindergarten	120 minutes a day	Centers/ free choice; also assigned by teacher	Appropriation
Martes	Kindergarten	30 minutes a week	Lab scheduled by teacher	Adoption
Robles/A	Kindergarten	30 minutes a day	Centers/ free choice	Adoption
Robles/B	Kindergarten	30 minutes a day	Centers/ free choice	Adoption
Bell	Kindergarten	20 minutes a day and 30– 60 minutes a week in computer lab	Centers/ scheduled by teacher to computer center once a week	Adaptation

[1]These levels of integration with curriculum and institution are drawn from Judith Sandholtz, Cathy Ringstaff, and David Dwyer, *Teaching with Technology* (New York: Teachers College Press, 1997), pp. 37–42. The levels are defined on pp. 122–123.

differences based on gender in access, use, or enthusiasm for the technologies.

In the preschools and kindergartens, many of the children working in the computer centers had brought to their tasks considerable fluency with home-based technologies. For example, at Jefferson preschool, the technologically enthusiastic Sherry Franklin (she had created a multimedia project of great artists' work for the class) was stumped by a question. One of us had noted that the Macintosh desktop screen was blue for boys and pink for girls and asked Franklin who had customized the colors on the desktop. She didn't know, and wanted to change the colors but didn't know how. She asked 4-year-old Gussie to change the colors; the child knew where the desktop settings were and told one of us what had to be done.

Students who were unfamiliar with booting up the computer, keyboarding, entering a password, and using a mouse stood aside as their neighbors with more expertise signed up often to play with the computer during center time. At the same time, home-users' fluency sometimes led to lack of interest. Four students told us that the software they used at school was the same they had at home; they would rather play with blocks or paint.

Teachers' Attitudes toward Technology

Of the ten teachers for whom we had data, eight had computers at home and used them extensively. The homeusers told us they spent at least an hour each week on the computer for personal business, preparing lessons, writing notes to parents, documenting children's work, emailing, and doing Internet searches. The majority had picked up their expertise with computers on their own, from a friend, or from a spouse. Only a handful had taken formal courses. Although a few expressed doubts about their competence with computers, their commitment to using technology in their classrooms often grew from their deep-seated belief in the importance of technology in their children's futures. These teachers, then, were hardly technophobes or allergic to using computers with young children.

All of the teachers believed that using computers was a worthwhile developmental activity for children, but mostly as an enrichment activity or as a learning tool rather than as a central task for their children to perform. Except for the five who worked at integrating the technology directly into the existing curriculum and teaching tasks, the teachers did not blend computers into the rest of the children's day. Only a few could troubleshoot computer problems. When a mouse was broken or software crashed, two of the teachers said that they could fix it themselves. The lack of technical support, except for the federally funded program described above, meant that the teachers depended on their own limited knowledge or the knowledge of parents to repair machines. In one Head Start center, the computer had gone unused for three months because the mouse was defective.

When we asked the teachers whether using computers had changed their teaching, five said that it had made no difference at all and four said that it made "some" to "major" differences in how they taught. We asked the four teachers, Rodrigues and Hunter among them, what kind of changes it had made in their classrooms. Their answers included adding a center, creating a multimedia project, and using their home computer to communicate with peers and parents and to prepare for the next day.

ment which is attractive and in good repair and includes such basic learning materials as hardwood . . . blocks and wooden floor toys."[26]

Since 1990, books and pamphlets have been published describing the use of computers in Head Start for both children and their parents. The Bureau issues bulletins advising staff of appropriate software and experts' opinions on how to use the new technologies. In 1988, for example, four early childhood experts offered their advice. Two said computers were fine to use in preschools as long as "developmentally appropriate goals and methods" are used; one said that the technology was fine for 5-year-olds but less appropriate for "3's or 4's." One expert emphatically said that the software programs available then for young children were "limited and unimaginative" and unequal to the "rich and complex experience of children's play."[27]

Since then, early childhood experts have remained divided. Contrary to technology vendors' claims and parental hopes that the earlier children are exposed to computers, the better it is, the veteran educational psychologist Jane Healy has stated flatly that before age 7, time spent with computers "not only subtracts from important developmental tasks but may also entrench bad learning habits, leading to poor motivation and even symptoms of learning disability."[28]

To support her claim—note the "may" in the sentence—Healy cites the brain development literature and what intellectual tasks children under age 7 need to accomplish: learning to use all the senses, paying attention, visualizing, memorizing, thinking logically, and understanding new symbol systems such as written words and numbers. For children younger than 7, navigating software with little understanding of what they are doing, she argues, deprives children of the exploration and play they need to grow intellectually. This is, of course, a caution for any activity done with any learning tool. Young children often misinterpret what happens with computers: "Can a computer cheat at tic-tac-toe?" a researcher asks a child. "Yes, it's alive, it cheats, but it doesn't know it's cheating."[29]

David Elkind, professor of Child Study at Tufts University, points out that parents and educators easily confuse a toddler's facility with language with the child's intellectual understanding of the large words they use or the complex sentences they construct. Parents and educators also jump to the conclusion that manipulating icons on the screen means that a child understands the actions and the symbols.[30] Coming from a different angle but making a similar point, the Harvard psychologist Jerome Kagan argues against the "infant determinists." The concept of a critical period of learning, a crucial window opened for a short time that slams shut after a certain age, he says, is "seductive" but inaccurate. He points to findings from studies on orphans who were adopted at a young age or children who had suffered deprivation for two to four years and then were put under the care of patient, nurturing foster parents or other adults; these children developed the typical emotional and intellectual vitality of others their age. He stresses the malleability of children and the importance of later developmental periods in the lives of children and adults.[31] For those educators and parents who fear that exposure to computers is rushing children through Piagetian stages of development, researcher Douglas Clements approvingly cites another researcher: "Children do not universally wake up on their seventh birthdays . . . to find that they have arrived at the period of concrete operations."[32] In short, waiting until later in childhood to introduce computers will not stunt children's intellectual, emotional, and social development.

Most researchers, however, believe in early childhood as a critical period for becoming literate, and they have few doubts about either the appropriateness or effectiveness of young children in preschools or kindergartens working on computers with software matched to their age. Some draw heavily from neuroscientists' work on the rapid increase in synapse formation— brain connectivity—in the womb and postnatal development to support policies that import hardware and software into preschools and kindergartens. Others, committed to the crucial influence of an enriched, complex environment on a child's development, conduct studies of technology uses in early childhood settings.[33]

Clements, for example, in two separate syntheses of research findings (1987 and 1993), concluded that computers are "developmentally appropriate for young children." In his 1987 conclusions, Clements expressed hesitation about the effects of computers on preschoolers and kindergartners: "Young children do not need computers any more than they 'need' any of many potentially valuable learning centers. There is, however, nothing to lose and potentially rich benefits to acquire through informed use of computers. Informed, because inappropriate or insipid uses will have little or no benefit. Effectiveness depends critically on the quality of the software, the amount of time it is used, and the way in which it is used."[34]

Five years later, however, the conditional language had disappeared. Faster computers, greater storage capacity, and better software may account for the change. Clements's review of new research in the late 1980s and early 1990s had convinced him of the effectiveness of computers for young children. "Appropriate computer programs can contribute to early childhood education. Young children use computers successfully and confidently, in balance with other activities. They prefer to control programs that are animated, problem solving-oriented, and interactive . . . Girls and boys, when young, do not differ in computer use, leading to recommendations that preschool is a good time to introduce moderate, safe use of this technology."[35]

Few researchers, however, examine closely what individual young children do when facing a screen and what sense they make of the written words, animation, and clever graphics that interactive software makers have brought elegantly to the current generation of computers. Popular stories that in a pre-computer age early childhood teachers would read to their children during circle-time, for example, have been made into "talking" CD-ROMs that are bought by districts and sent to classrooms.

Linda Labbo studied a kindergarten boy of average ability who interacted with two talking CD-ROMS to see to what degree the child understood the story after interacting with the software. She found that there were so many distracting multimedia features to "Arthur's Teacher Trouble" that Roberto could not retell the story in a coherent, structured way. Yet "Stellaluna," another talking CD-ROM story about a baby bat, was sufficiently structured for Roberto to tell the researchers a coherent story about the adventures of a mother bat and her babies.[36]

Labbo's point is that teachers who lack the time to preview software for their classes—were they even to be asked to do so—believed that popular stories on talking CD-ROMS would help their children learn more about stories and characters. Yet significant differences in the structure of the story and use of multimedia features had differential outcomes in one boy's understanding of two stories. I offer this extended example of the importance of on-site research with children and teachers to get at the varied effects of software products on teaching and learning.

For parents seeking a clear answer to the question of how early, if at all, infants and toddlers should be exposed to computers, experts and researchers offer little comfort. Professional educators offer little more. Not until 1996 did the National Association of Education for Young Children (NAEYC) publish guidelines for the use of computers in early childhood programs. Knowing about Head Start's moratorium on computer purchases in 1984 and the subsequent cautious embrace of a two-computer-per-center solution in 1990, NAEYC's statements acknowledged both their concerns and the positive effects of technology on children's learning. Their position paper, citing Douglas Clements's research syntheses, also recognized the potentially harmful effects of particular software products and too much reliance on technology.

Far short of an enthusiastic endorsement of computers in early childhood classrooms, the NAEYC position accepts the ubiquity of computers in society and the futility of trying to stem a technological tide with mere words. The organization's statement concluded: "In any given situation, a professional judgment by the teacher is required to determine if a specific use of technology is age appropriate, individually appropriate, and culturally appropriate."[37] It is the teacher, using computers or other information technologies as learning tools, who can, if so inclined, integrate the machines into the classroom.

So the answer of practitioners, academics, and researchers to the question of whether computers should be used in preschools and kindergartens is a tentative, highly conditional yes, surrounded by a thicket of qualifiers. No substantial body of evidence is yet available to either confirm the high hopes or ease the troubling concerns of parents and educators about whether too much or too little academic preparation, too much or too little technology, is good for young children.

Aside from the general lack of evidence concerning young children's experience using computers, there remains the pervasive belief among educators and parents about the inevitability of a future in which today's children will require technological competencies to succeed in the workplace. It is that belief, and not any research findings, that propels parents and educators to invest in preschools and computers.[38]

The actual use of the machines and programs that we found in preschools and kindergartens in the heart of Silicon Valley mirrors that belief, along with a core faith in the power of schooling to shape a child's destiny. When computers were deployed as just another activity center in ten of the eleven sites, the machines were used infrequently. Such marginal use reflects a combination of factors, ranging from lack of sustained technical support to uncertainty about what sorts of activities advance or impede development among preschoolers. Since none of the eleven teachers we studied were technophobes, their use of computers as no more or less than just another learning center suggests that the traditional purposes of preschool and kindergarten will continue as before, even with the presence of computer stations in the classroom. Despite the claims of technology promotors that computers can transform teaching and learning, the teachers we studied adapted computers to sustain, rather than transform, their philosophy that the whole child develops best when both work and play are cultivated and "developmentally appropriate" tasks and activities are offered. The seven sites that we studied taught us a straightforward lesson: even with their limited use of technology, these preschools and kindergartens seek primarily to conserve traditional civic, academic, and social values rather than turn children into future Net-workers.

Many parents in Silicon Valley, especially single ones, feel overwhelmed by the economic and emotional stresses of working one or more jobs and parenting one or more children in a fast-paced world where a parent's job is seldom secure and civic responsibilities seem remote. Preschools and kindergartens at our sites, even ones with a clear academic tilt, seem to offer the continuity, care, attention, character building, and stimulation that traditional families once offered children at home. The bonds that grow between 4-year-olds and their teacher are like the ones that grow in close families, but because of contemporary pressures these bonds are too often partial or even missing at home. Such bonds seldom evolve from child-machine interactions.

Listening to teachers and parents talk about children and computers taught us anew how crucial the preschool and kindergarten are to fortifying the civic, social, and emotional lives of both children and parents, many of whom are leading helter-skelter lives regardless of socioeconomic background. These eleven classrooms were a safe haven, a friendly place that supplied the stability and caregiving often truncated in contemporary family life. These teachers and their activities promoted continuity in children's and parents' lives rather than deep changes.

Putting computers into classroom centers conveyed to parents the powerful symbolism of the electronic revolution; their limited use in reality mattered little in these preschool and kindergarten programs. Regardless of which version of goodness a program pursued, the teachers opted for building emotional, social, and intellectual ties that reached well beyond proficiency with machines. If anything, the "computer center" unintentionally sustained the traditional early childhood school model—despite the insistent efforts of some to push academics for 3-year-olds. And that is the ultimate irony. In pressing early childhood teachers to use computers with eye-catching software for tykes, zealous parents and educators have not transformed preschools and kindergartens into new and different versions of "good schools. Rather, they have watched a technological innovation get reinvented into a benign addition to traditional early childhood programs.[39]

3

HIGH-TECH SCHOOLS, LOW-TECH LEARNING

Shelley, an eleventh grader in Alison Piro's humanities class, is standing on a raised platform in the middle of the classroom, surrounded by students seated at their group tables. The classroom lights are turned off and the shades are drawn. The only light in the room comes from the overhead projector, which Alison Piro positions to spotlight Shelley. With these words, "The freedom we should demand," Shelley begins her speech as ex-slave Frederick Douglass.[1]

These few moments in Piro's classroom capture the essence of her teaching—dramatic, diligently planned, and even innovative in its use of technology (albeit in this case a low-tech machine). The environment is warm and safe and conducive to students' performances. Whether it is a literary reading, a film produced by students, a piece of sculpture, or a slide show, performance is a central part of Piro's pedagogy, a strategy she believes allows students to demonstrate their comprehension of concepts and themes they have read and discussed. In Shelley's case it is the reworking of ideas from Frederick Douglass's autobiography into a powerful speech on freedmen's rights. Piro's use of the overhead projector to spotlight Shelley's performance illustrates her innovative approach to technology in the classroom.

A teacher with five years' experience, Alison Piro teaches two periods of an eleventh-grade interdisciplinary humanities class each day and works the rest of the day to help create a standards-based curriculum for ninth graders. She co-plans and coordinates the block schedule humanities class with Alan Bloom. He takes the lead on social studies curriculum, and she takes the lead on English curriculum, though both agree that it is entirely a team effort. Each class has 32 students.

Piro is a leader in the school in integrating curriculum across disciplines, as well as a leader in integrating computers into that interdisciplinary curriculum. She believes in the power of technology as a teaching and learning tool and wants to tap its potential. "It's how you use the tool," Piro says. "If we are only using it to word-process then we may as well have typewriters."

Piro has integrated computers into the humanities curriculum in numerous ways. Students access the Internet to do research, and they use word-processing programs to write passages that accompany visual presentations. These include slide shows done on Claris Works and films made with AVID software. She expects students to "conceptualize and actualize" ideas using technology as the medium. For example, after reading several works in utopian literature, groups of students had to create their own utopias and make a film (using AVID software) that would "sell" their utopias to their audience, their classmates.[2]

Piro sees three ways that information technology can be beneficial to her students: by granting them direct access to facts, ideas, and primary sources; by linking images and concepts to sound and film, allowing students to produce creative and professional presentations rather than collages on posterboard; and by motivating students, especially those who would not otherwise be engaged. For instance, almost all of her students came in on an optional Saturday to work on their utopia projects. "I could teach what I want without computers, but not with the outcomes I want. The visual presentation wouldn't be possible without the use of technology now. We do a lot of performing. All it takes to perform is people. But it is so beautiful to cast an image behind the people performing. Or to have music, or a piece of text coming through."

Piro's students use computers in school up to eight times a month. Typically students work in pairs or groups on projects that take up to two weeks. This method puts Piro in the role of facilitator, moving from group to group to support and challenge them as they proceed. "Our technology use tends to span several days. For instance, when we were doing our utopian society project, we were in the media center, using butcher paper, pencils, and pens for about three days before we ever got to the technology. Then we spent a whole day researching images on laser disk, video, and the Internet. Then we spent a whole other three days and a Saturday working with AVID. So there are levels of technology use that get us to the point where we are actually manipulating the hardware and software."

Piro contends that through the use of computers students can demonstrate their knowledge and show whether they reach the school standards that teachers have set. Computers, however, are not appropriate for all projects. It depends, Piro emphasizes, on what the teaching and learning goals are. She admits that at times she has chosen incorrectly. An essay, for example, may have been a more appropriate assignment than a computer project.

Alison Piro is a thoughtful, determined teacher who carefully considers what tool—an essay, a computerized slide show, a short answer exam, a piece of art, a digitized movie, a research project using the Internet—is most appropriate to engage students. Technology, like an essay in English class, is integral to helping her achieve her teaching goals.

Piro and a handful of other teachers in two Silicon Valley high schools represent teachers who have fully integrated technology into their daily instruction. According to national surveys and reports, technology leaders like Piro make up a tiny fraction of school faculties; they are the early adopters of technological innovations. In national data they differ greatly from their colleagues both in the frequency with which they use computers in their classrooms and in the ways they teach. Across the country, most teachers and their students are nonusers or occasional-to-rare users of these machines in classrooms.[3] Furthermore, when teachers do use computers for instruction, another unexpected outcome emerges, again derived from national data but apparent in the schools we studied. When teachers adopt technological innovations, these changes typically maintain rather than alter existing classroom practices.[4]

FREQUENCY AND TYPE OF TECHNOLOGY USE
IN SCHOOLS AND CLASSROOMS

Fifteen years ago, I found that the vast majority of U.S. teachers were nonusers of computers in their classrooms, about 1 in 4 was an occasional user (at least once a month), and 1 in 10 was a serious user (at least one or more times a week). At a time when access to hardware and software was quite limited we would expect such minimal use. National data then and since largely confirmed that claim.[5]

Since the early 1990s, however, wiring schools, buying vast

amounts of hardware and software, and campaigning to convince teachers to use new technologies in their classrooms have produced a modest shift from nonusers to occasional users and from occasional users to serious ones. Yet even with this modest shift in reported classroom use, over half of elementary and middle school teachers continue to be nonusers of computers for classroom instruction, about 1 in 3 are occasional users, and about 1 in 10 uses the technologies daily. According to a survey of computer coordinators, elementary school students spent about 1 3/4 hours per week in labs and classrooms using computers. But when students themselves were surveyed, they reported much less computer time: fifth graders said about 24 minutes a week and eighth graders reported 38 minutes a week. In the high school, 2 of 10 teachers report being serious users, and 4 of 10 report using machines at least once a month. The rest never use technologies in classrooms. So over the last decade there has been some movement among elementary teachers from nonusers to occasional ones and a modest shift toward occasional and serious use in high schools.[6]

Although we need to know how often students turn on computers in school, we also need to know what they do when the screen lights up. Teachers and senior high school students across the country report they use machines mostly for word processing. Among eighth-grade math teachers, less than half reported in 1996 that they used computers at all. Of those teachers who did, 18 percent said their students use drill-and-practice software, 13 percent said students play math games, another 13 percent of teachers said their students do simulations, and 5 percent used software to demonstrate new concepts in math.[7] In the end, both supporters and critics of school technology (including researchers) have claimed that powerful software and hardware often get used in limited ways to simply maintain rather than transform prevailing instructional practices.

What I find in the national data is far too much reliance on self-reports and far less investigation of actual use in local schools. Thus, Heather Kirkpatrick, Craig Peck, and I studied two Silicon Valley high schools to see if the national patterns were evident in settings where technologies were abundant and strongly advocated by public officials, educators, and parents. Two questions guided our inquiry:

- Given abundant access to information technologies, to what degree did the national patterns of infrequent and limited teacher use of computers emerge at the two high schools? If so, why?
- To what degree did teachers in the two high schools who used computers in their classrooms typically maintain existing practices? If so, why?[8]

LAS MONTAÑAS HIGH SCHOOL

Surrounded by hills that turn rich green in the winter and golden in the spring and summer (although cynical East Coast visitors call it brown), Las Montañas is located on 47 acres of prime property in the heart of Silicon Valley. In 1976, when Las Montañas opened its doors for the first time to 1,300 students, 58 teachers, and five administrators, there was little doubt that the high school was innovative. In an open-space building, its 160,000 square feet of carpeted, air-conditioned space housed a large media center and office suite in its core, as well as a Forum—a large open gathering place for students—two gyms, a cafeteria, snack bar, and faculty room. In addition to an array of regular classrooms, there were specialized rooms for music, drama, science, art, and vocational training. As enrollment grew over the years, portable classrooms were added and have since become fixtures outside the main building. Las Montañas also had a distinctive curriculum with an individualized program for its mostly college-bound clientele. Short courses, semester courses, and flexible weekly schedules gave students and teachers many options.[9] If curriculum and scheduling were unusual, so was school governance. The entire school was divided into three units, each with an administrator, one-third of the students from all grades, teachers from all academic subjects, and one secretary. Each unit was further subdivided into two "learning communities" led by a coordinator who was a teacher selected by both students and colleagues. In addition, every certified staff member, including the principal, advised a small group of students for 15 minutes a day. Every Wednesday morning the entire faculty would meet for updates on the week's issues and divide into their learning communities; school began one hour later and periods were shortened so that advisers could meet with their students toward the end of the school day.[10]

Beginning in the late 1970s, however, a series of events altered considerably the staffing and program at Las Montañas. California voters approved Proposition 13, which significantly reduced funding for schools in the early 1980s. The legislature mandated school reform in 1983, modifying further what could and could not be done in the state's high schools. Then in 1986 a federal court ordered busing throughout the district to reduce school segregation of Latinos and other minorities.

At about the same time, Silicon Valley was emerging as a national center of high-tech innovation, development, and production. Venture capitalists funded start-up companies that made multimillionaires out of 20-something engineers and programmers, and parents and business leaders pressured schools to adopt more technology. The state legislature and department of education responded with grants and technical support. Staff in most school districts, including the one in which Las Montañas was located, drew up technology plans for wiring schools, purchasing hardware and software, and deploying information technologies for instruction.

By the early 1990s, Las Montañas had changed considerably. Counselors had been let go, class sizes had ballooned, staff had turned over, flexible scheduling had dissolved. The governance arrangements were still in place but exerted little influence on what occurred in the school. More minority students now attended even as overall enrollment had declined. Moreover, standardized achievement test scores had slipped below the national average.

In 1992 a new principal arrived. Adrian Jones envisioned making Las Montañas a high-tech magnet school that would draw teachers and students from the entire district and stem the hemorrhaging enrollment and loss of effective teachers. Attracting technology-oriented teachers from other district schools as well as young, energetic first-year teachers, he succeeded at recruiting a cadre of young, reform-minded faculty intent on creating interdisciplinary programs that integrated information technologies into their daily work. Jones's success convinced district and state officials, foundations, and Silicon Valley entrepreneurs to invest in Las Montañas.

By the mid-1990s, about one-third of the faculty had created interdisciplinary programs within a school that the district called a technology magnet. Staff, business leaders, parents, and students had hammered out a mission statement, schoolwide goals, and specific curricular standards. Faultlines appeared among the faculty, however, as teachers argued over academic and disciplinary standards. Nonetheless, within five years, enrollments in interdisciplinary programs had gone from less than 10 percent in two grades to about 40 percent of students across all grades and academic subjects. New teachers sought out the school.[11]

By 1998–99, when my colleagues and I arrived to conduct our study, the reform-minded principal had left for a different post, his successor, committed to the same vision, had been on the job for two years, and the five-year magnet grant was ending. Under the new principal's administration, Las Montañas had received a major grant from a Bay Area reform group to be a "leadership" school in the region. In addition, a state Digital High School grant provided more hardware and wiring for the entire school.

Although the school's media center, technology, interdisciplinary programs, and jointly produced standards continued to be central to the new principal's plans for Las Montañas, she knew that many features of the program from a quarter-century ago had disappeared. Only two teachers, for example, remained from the original faculty. Furthermore, she and faculty leaders realized that although individual programs may shine, "teachers are generally not aware of standards that exist outside of their departments . . . [and] the efforts of individual programs have not been converted into systemic, schoolwide reform"—especially, she might have added, reforms that targeted improvements in students' academic performance.[12]

The state's Standardized Testing and Reporting (STAR) program, a mandated test (Stanford-9), had been used to measure ninth, tenth, and eleventh graders' academic performance in reading, math, language, science, and social science in the last two years. These results showed some improvements but overall scores were substantially below national averages. Furthermore, none of the statistics on student performance were broken out by ethnicity or race, therefore masking serious academic issues facing the faculty and administration. Chief among them are literacy and the numbers of minority students failing in each grade.

Faculty and administration, long aware of the academic deficiencies, have mobilized resources to attack the problem. Much attention had been given to implementing schoolwide standards established in 1994, further expanding interdisciplinary programs, restructuring the ninth grade to help students perform better academically, and intensifying efforts to apply technology to teaching and learning. The state Digital High School grant, for example, focuses on the ninth grade interdisciplinary core program, which includes a required course in "computer productivity."[13]

Table 3. Las Montañas Star Results for 1998 and 1999[1]

Grade	Reading		Math		Language		Science		Social science	
	1998	1999	1998	1999	1998	1999	1998	1999	1998	1999
9	28	37	48	55	45	48	37	39	44	33
10	25	32	39	49	37	38	37	41	35	37
11	31	34	44	53	41	48	39	41	53	48

[1]Figures are stated in national percentiles.
Source: *Bay Area News,* July 7, 1999, p. 6A.

FLATLAND HIGH SCHOOL

Exiting a freeway somewhere between San Francisco and San Jose, we approach Flatland High School—a familiar scene to most people who have attended high schools elsewhere in the United States. Rounding a corner, one sees the athletic fields with their light stanchions, the highest landmark on the 33-acre site. The new science wing, under construction (which will contain a computer lab), blends in well with the buff-colored two-story main building constructed in 1961. On the main campus, classrooms, auditorium, gyms, and faculty rooms surround a large, paved square with tables and benches where students congregate during breaks throughout the day. North of the main campus, along a creek, are buildings housing mostly vocational classrooms with antiquated equipment—relics of the school's original purpose. Built forty years earlier, the high school's primary mission had been to train students for the workplace. Flatland was the district's vocational high school. By contrast, the first high school built in the district—locals called it the "mother" school—had served students journeying toward both college and the workplace. After Flatland was built, the mother high school specialized even more in preparing students for higher education. As has happened in school districts across the nation, students felt the social class differences within the two schools' populations, and this sensitivity often expressed itself in rivalries between athletic teams and disagreements among students and teachers over which school—the blue-collar or white-collar one—was better.

For the last two decades, however, state and national school reforms affecting Flatland have shifted its vocational orientation considerably. Now it seeks to prepare most students for two- and four-year colleges and universities, although the school retained some vocational offerings under the title of school-to-career programs. Entrepreneurial district administrators secured state grants for innovations, including technology, and have planned extensively for district-wide technology use by wiring schools, providing technical support, and purchasing new computers and software.[14]

The current principal, Randy Astor, taught at Flatland in the early 1980s and went on to become an administrator at the mother high school for four years before returning to Flatland as principal in 1991. Astor has sought out partnerships with local firms to bring equipment, software, and help into the school. He sees as his role expanding the horizons of the mostly minority students to include education beyond high school and building a technological infrastructure that will support greater use of computers and other information technologies by teachers and students inside and outside of classrooms.[15]

Flatland serves almost 1,900 students. Over the last decade, the school population had grown larger and more culturally diverse. Most Flatland students are now minority and range from low- to middle-income families. Just under one-fourth of the students are eligible for free and reduced-cost lunch. In 1998 and 1999 the STAR test results for Flatland, compared with national averages, were disappointing to the school staff (see Table 4). Furthermore, the absence of a breakdown of test scores by ethnicity or race obscures serious academic issues facing the faculty and administration, such as overall student literacy. Teacher comments reveal that large numbers of students, particularly minority students who speak and read English as their second language, had fallen behind in literacy skills. These numbers, troubling to the administration and faculty, have led

Table 4. Flatland Star Results for 1998 and 1999[1]

Grade	Reading		Math		Language		Science		Social science	
	1998	1999	1998	1999	1998	1999	1998	1999	1998	1999
9	37	41	55	61	58	58	45	50	46	47
10	32	37	50	54	46	49	46	50	42	43
11	37	39	53	57	50	52	44	47	59	61

[1]The figures are stated in national percentiles.
Source: *Bay Area News*, July 7, 1999, p. 6A.

to schoolwide initiatives aimed at restructuring the ninth grade into faculty teams that plan for cross-subject teaching, special classes in academic subjects for Limited English Proficiency (LEP) students, and harnessing new technologies to help students become more literate.[16]

Three accreditation reports (1991, 1994, and 1997) concur that Flatland faculty and administration have worked hard to offer a blend of programs for students seeking various career paths following graduation. For students primarily interested in entry-level jobs in local industries—but not only such students—there are the Electronics Academy, Culinary Arts Hospitality and Management Program, Computer-Assisted Drafting, Information Systems (computer repair and construction), Automotive Technology, and a partnership program with a major local computer firm that provides professionals, equipment, and software for students to prepare for entry-level jobs. For those who intend to enroll in colleges and universities, there are honors and advanced placement offerings in most academic subjects. So Flatland High School, once *the* vocational school in the district, has moved aggressively toward becoming a full-fledged comprehensive high school offering a wide range of courses to students seeking higher education or a direct route into entry-level posts in technology firms a mile or two away. Still, beginnings matter. The tug of Flatland's vocational school legacy can still be felt in the facilities, the partnerships, and the array of work-related school programs, just as Las Montañas' legacy of innovation remains (see Table 5).[17] These two four-year high schools in the middle of Silicon Valley have similar per-pupil expenditures, culturally and socioeconomically diverse student populations, and students who aspire to higher education. In academic performance, as measured by standardized tests, the results are roughly the same, although Flatland's

Table 5. Comparison of Two Silicon Valley High Schools, 1999

Item	Flatland	Las Montañas
Total number of students	1854	1262
Total teaching staff	81	60
Diversity of students/teachers (%)		
Latinos	24/18	39/11
Whites	40/76	26/83
Asian/Pacific Islanders	32/4	20/2
African American	3/1	10/2
Percentage of students receiving free/reduced lunch	27	44
Percentage of limited English proficient students	14	16
Combined average SAT scores	999	1013
Percentage of graduates planning to attend community college/university	55/30[1]	40/32[1]
Per-pupil expenditure	$5178	$5263

[1]Data are for 1997.

scores on the state test are closer to national norms than those of Las Montañas. The two schools are also similar in making available to students and teachers the latest information technologies, as we will see.

Access to Computers and Other Technologies

The common metric to judge public schools' response to the massive technological changes of the last quarter-century is the ratio of students to computers. The calculation is done by dividing a school's total number of students by its total number of computers. Since the early 1980s, acquiring more machines to reduce the ratio has been the primary measure of a school's technological progress. Nationally, the figures show sharp reductions, from 92 students per computer in public schools in 1983–84, to 27 per computer five years later, to just under 6 students for each computer in 1999. The numbers represent a staggering financial investment in just over fifteen years.[18]

The number of schools and classrooms wired for Internet access has become another measure of technological innovation. In 1994, 35 percent of U.S. schools were connected to the Internet. Wiring of at least one site in each building increased to 90 percent in 1999. In 1994, 3 percent of all classrooms were connected to the Internet; a mere three years later, 27 percent had been wired.[19]

A third measure of access to computers is the variety in placement of computers among media centers, computer labs, and individual classrooms. As Tables 6 and 7 make clear, in the two districts and high schools we studied, district and high school administrators made determined efforts to wire classrooms, purchase high-end computers, and distribute them to various locations within the school.[20]

Table 6. Students per Computer, by Location, 1998–1999

Location	Nation	California	Flatland	Las Montañas
Schoolwide	6	6	5	4
Classrooms	17	22	22	17
Labs	21	318	12	NA
Library	114	185	109	16

Table 7. Internet Connectivity, 1997–1998

Percent connected	Nation	California	Flatland	Las Montañas
Classrooms	44	44	64	80
Labs	54	55	80	100
Libraries	70	50	100	100
Schools where teachers have email[1]	39	35	100	100

[1]Percentage is calculated for those schools that have at least 50 percent of their teachers with email addresses.

Missing from the tables is information on the number of district courses offered, the number of days set aside for teacher training, and the amount of release time for teachers and administrators. Also absent are descriptions of the on-site technical support by designated teachers and their cadre of highly skilled student assistants. Nonetheless, by most available measures, both of these high schools would easily be described as technology-rich, except for placement of computers in classrooms.

In our study we also asked teachers and students whether they had computers at home, how often they used them, and what uses they made of them. We found that home use by students and teachers was frequent and spanned many applications, exceeding both students' and teachers' uses during classroom instruction (see Tables 8, 9, and 10).

Teacher Use

We turn now to our first question: Given the abundant access to information technologies afforded teachers and students at the schools, to what degree did teachers actually use the available computers for instruction and in what way were they used? Teachers used computers in similar ways in the two schools (see

Table 8. Percentage of Students and Teachers with Computers at Home, 1999

Group	Flatland	Las Montañas	National
Students	85	90 (1997)[1]	56
Teachers	76	85 (1998)[2]	80

[1]U.S. Department of Commerce, Bureau of the Census, *Current Population Survey,* October 1997, unpublished data, table 425, p. 482.
[2]Henry Becker, Jason Ravitz, YanTien Wong, "Teacher and Teacher-Directed Student Use of Computers and Software," Report #3, Center for Research on Information Technology and Organizations, University of California, Irvine, and The University of Minnesota, November 1999, p. 35.

Table 9. Frequency of Home Use in Two High Schools, 1999

	Flatland		Las Montañas	
Frequency	Students	Teachers	Students	Teachers
At least once a week	82%	86%	84%	67%
At least once a month	13%	7%	13%	10%
No use	5%	7%	2%	NA

Table 11). At both schools, each classroom had one computer for the teacher's use. There were five labs in Flatland and ten labs in Las Montañas, and well-stocked media centers at each school. In the schools we studied, teachers reported that they largely used school computers to prepare for classes rather than for direct instructional use.

Consider the experience of Hector Diaz, a ninth grader at

Table 10. Types of Home Use of Computers Reported by Teachers, 1999

Use	Flatland	Las Montañas
Personal use	76%	85%
Prepare school materials	72%	73%
Use email	71%	NA
Search Internet	64%	NA
Prepare tests	63%	65%
Prepare lesson plans	57%	58%

Sources: All figures for Flatland teachers come from a survey administered at an in-service meeting in April 1999. The response rate was 77 percent. Las Montañas results from a survey in October 1998. Response rate was 83 percent.

Table 11. Types of Computer Use at School Reported by Teachers, 1999

Use	Flatland	Las Montañas	National[1]
Word processing	71%	76%	NA
Recording grades	56%	59%	58%
Email	51%	85%	NA
Searching Internet	47%	68%	24%

[1]National figures are for 1998 and are taken from Henry Becker, Jason Ravitz, YanTien Wong, *Teaching, Learning, and Computing: 1998 National Survey,* Center for Research on Information Technology and Organizations, University of California, Irvine, and The University of Minnesota, November 1999, p. 32. I averaged percentages for four academic subjects that were reported in the study.

Las Montañas. I went with Hector to four of his classes one early December day. After introducing myself to the teacher, I sat in the back of each classroom to observe, and on our way to the next class, Hector and I would discuss what had just occurred. Over lunch, we talked further about his courses, the computer at home that he used every night, and other aspects of school. Because he was on the soccer team and there was a game that day, I did not see his English and science classes.

French I had 29 students in the class. Between 7:50 A.M. and 8:45 A.M., the teacher taught the whole group using a lesson in the text (*Discovering French*) and one-page handouts of a dialogue between two people. She asked seven pairs of students to come to the front of the room to read aloud the two parts of the dialogue. About half of the class was engaged, and the others were doing homework for other classes, quietly talking, or staring into space. The teacher occasionally said "shhhhh" to get silence for those students reading the dialogue at the front of the room.

On our way to Hector's second-period class, I asked him if the French class was typical. He nodded yes. "I block out the noise," he said. I asked about the one computer in the classroom, and Hector explained that it was the teacher's and she used it to record grades. They had used computers, he added, in the media center for a class project on France. He had used Photoshop software at school because he had it at home.

The math class was using an experimental curriculum that required each student to use a graphing calculator. Today was a test. Because the teacher was at a math conference, a substitute administered the scheduled test. Students could use their calculators and note cards. The sub gave directions for the test and the next assignment. She expected students who finished the test before the bell rang to begin the homework. Hector had prepared for the test. The one computer in the classroom was used solely by the teacher for recording grades, according to Hector. The class had not been to any of the computer labs or to the media center during the semester.

In art class, each student was working on a project that grew out of a video portraying a graffiti artist using vivid colors to protest social injustices. Each student had to create a personal statement about an issue using techniques that the graffiti artist had used. For 45 minutes, the teacher moved among the tables asking and answering questions about each project. Some students pinned up their work on a wall, stepped back to look at it, asking a classmate for a critique, took it down, and returned to their tables to do more work. Hector was absorbed completely in his painting until the teacher announced in the last five minutes that it was time to clean up and put the materials away. I asked the teacher about the one computer in the room. She said that she used it for administrative tasks. She had not used any of the computer labs or the media center thus far in the semester.

In the core course that combined English and History, the social studies teacher carried on a whole-group discussion for a half-hour to introduce inductive and deductive reasoning. She used many concrete examples drawn from students' lives and current events in the nation and world. Virtually all of the students paid attention, listened to one another, and engaged in the discussion. Hector contributed to the discussion once. Next, the teacher asked the class to take out a sheet of paper and write down two examples of inductive reasoning not used in the class, and two of deductive reasoning. After waiting for students to jot down their examples, the teacher assigned each student a partner. Each pair were to review their examples and give feedback to one another on the accuracy and clarity of the examples. The teacher went over to two students who had been talking quietly most of the period and asked them to leave. She spoke with them in the hallway and they returned chastened and plunged into the task. Ten minutes before the end of the period, the teacher asked the class to stop and sought volunteers among the pairs to give their examples. A whole-group discussion ensued that assessed the strengths and weaknesses of the examples until the bell rang ending the period. As students were packing to leave, the teacher assigned students to observe and write down five examples of each form of reasoning. Hector told me that today's class was typical of the rest of the week.

I had noticed a cart in the room holding a VCR, monitor, and four computers. I asked Hector about the machines and he told me that the class had seen a video this week. From time to time, he said, some students would use the computers in class to do Internet searches on topics being discussed. He said that for this class he would use his computer at home to complete the homework.

Two of Hector's teachers used computers occasionally, one of whom used the media center. Many teachers in both schools also took their students to the media centers, where there were enough machines to accommodate an entire classroom for one or more periods. The data we collected from each center show that half to three-quarters of the teachers used the media center (see Table 12).

The numbers above, however, cannot bear close scrutiny. A minority of teachers (25 percent in one school, 32 percent in the other) in three departments (English, science, and social studies) accounted for 60–70 percent of all machine use in both schools' media centers. Furthermore, when the teacher-users

Table 12. Teacher Use of High School Media Centers

Item	Flatland 1997–1998	Flatland 1998–1999	Las Montañas 1998–1999
Percentage of faculty who brought classes to the center	55	48	74
Median number of days teachers who brought classes to the center used computers	4	5	12
Median percentage of yearly instructional time	3	3	8
Median number of periods teachers used computers in the center	9	8.5	34
Median percentage of yearly instructional time	1	1	5

whose primary duty was actually to teach students how to use computers—in classes on keyboarding, multimedia, and business applications—are subtracted from the total, a tiny band of academic subject teachers account for most machine use in these settings. In other words, two-thirds to three-quarters of the teachers who taught academic subjects in both schools were largely nonusers of the media centers' resources. Furthermore, data from students' and teachers' interviews and from surveys of staffs in both schools reinforced the basic point that there was a general lack of teacher technology use for instruction in classrooms and labs elsewhere in the schools, not just in the media centers.

Student Use

We shadowed 12 students one day each at Flatland and Las Montañas, covering each grade level and all of the schools' academic subjects. In these classes we observed 35 different teachers (one-quarter of both faculties). On randomly chosen days, we observed that nine of the 35 teachers (in computer courses, social studies, and humanities—integrated English and social studies—classes) had students keyboarding, searching the Internet, and working on projects at the computer. The other 26 teachers in social studies, science, English, math, and foreign language used a familiar teaching repertoire: lecture, review of homework, recitation, and whole-group discussion. Four of the 26 used slides, videos, or overhead projectors for part of the periods we observed.

We interviewed 33 students, including the 12 we shadowed. They reported serious to occasional use of computers and other technologies (including videos, television, laser disc players, and overhead projectors) in particular courses (some in English and social studies, but mostly in tech-heavy classes such as business, drafting, multimedia, and computer networking at various grade levels). For the majority of their academic classes, however, students reported little to no use of computers for instruction, but did mention occasional videos, television programs, and overhead projectors.

Based on what we saw and what teachers and students reported, we concluded that the integration of computers into classroom curricula and instruction techniques was minimal. It ranged from entry level to adoption, with fewer than five at the adaptation level. We noted only four academic teachers in both schools (excluding those teachers designated to teach computer classes) who effortlessly and continually used technology in their classes, that is, appropriated it as part of their weekly work.[21]

Finally, in a survey of about one-quarter of each school's enrollment, representing every academic subject and covering all grades in the high school, students reported some computer use in English and social studies and little to no use in math, science, and foreign language. Moreover, the kinds of use students reported were typing up assignments, working on reports, and searching the Internet. These results converge with the other data we have analyzed from national reports.

There was as much variation within a department as there was between departments. In the English Department, one or two teachers were especially heavy users of computers, a few were occasional to rare users, and the rest were largely nonusers. This pattern was similar across departments.

There were a handful of students, however, whose in-school lives changed with increased access to technology. We called them "open-door" students (their computer competence enhanced their desire to do well in school and hence opened doors to learning) and "tech gods" (students recognized by adults and fellow students for their substantial expertise).[22] Open-door students were predominately, though not exclusively, male and from varied ethnic backgrounds. Whether aided by family and friends or self-taught, all had gained their expertise outside of school, usually on home computers. As one student explained, "I started with my Dad's Atari, then moved to his 486 in sixth grade . . . Learning on your own is better." Another added that he had gained little experience at school, but "a lot at home." Each also reported that they were heavy home users, whether engaging in complex tasks such as trouble-shooting and programming or simply completing their homework. All were aware that their use of computers, both in and out of school, exceeded by a large measure that of most of their classmates.

Individual open-door students were quite candid about the importance of having access to computers in schools. "It's an outlet," one student said, "where I am good at something, where I can produce good work and get good feedback." Another student simply said: "I am good at computers so I am good at school." Though small in numbers (teachers at each school were able to identify at most ten such students), open-door students seemed to find not only satisfaction in using school technology but had gained much confidence in themselves.

Many of the open-door students went on to use their technological expertise to help their schools innovate. As one of these self-anointed "tech gods" explained: "I like seeing how people look stupid when they don't know what they are doing on the computer. I say, 'This is how you do it,' and they go 'Thank you, you are my god.' It makes me feel good."

Having student computer experts on hand was clearly vital to both high schools. First, students with particular expertise fortified the schools' small number of technologically proficient teachers. A few Flatland students in a technology-using social studies teacher's class created a web club that helped the teacher keep the school's site filled with compelling, up-to-date content. One tech god reported that he had helped a science teacher create a program to monitor what sites his students were surfing.

Moreover, tech gods helped ease the demand placed upon a school's technology support team which, as in most schools nationwide, was understaffed and overburdened. At Flatland, the official support staff consisted of one teacher who also taught three classes; at Las Montañas, it consisted of one full-time tech coordinator. After considering their heavy job demands (establish the school's network, maintain its 300 or so computers, write grants for new equipment, determine the school's technology policies), the coordinators cultivated cadres of technologically proficient students to help them keep the machines running. Though numbering only about five students in each school, these techies-in-arms helped the coordinators with various tasks from the mundane (finding a cable) to the essential (routing a network).[23]

Clearly then, there were segments of the school's population greatly affected by increased access to technology, especially the open-door students and tech gods who joined other students attracted to advanced technology-based electives. Further, students in classes taught by teachers who have become serious users received a technology-enhanced academic experience. Taken together, however, we estimate that these students represented at most 5 percent of the total student population, making them a small exception rather than a rule.[24]

What was true at both schools was also true nationally. After two decades during which U.S. presidents, corporate executives, and educational policymakers extravagantly promoted new and powerful technologies, most teachers and students now have far more access than previously, but classroom use continues to be uneven and infrequent.

MAXIMAL ACCESS, MINIMAL CHANGE

We have presented data from two high schools to elaborate the high access and limited use. Next we turn to another outcome and the question that it presented: Did teachers in the high schools who used computers in their classrooms typically maintain or alter their core teaching practices?

In interviews with the 21 teachers, 13 (just over 60 percent) said that their teaching had indeed changed because of their use of information technologies. Most of those who said they had changed mentioned: planning more efficiently, communicating with colleagues and parents far more often via email, and securing education materials from the Internet. Second, they highlighted the importance of having an additional tool in their customary set of teaching practices. Finally, they saw students' access to information—via the worldwide library represented by the Internet—as a phenomenal enhancement to their teaching.

A young social studies teacher who said that using technology has changed his teaching explained:

> The technology has just given me more tools to use . . . One thing I think it has allowed me to do is to access certain students who need something kinetic . . . Like the students who made the video aren't the kind of students who are going to write and debate the question: Does democracy really exist? Because there are other students who can debate with so much more power that they are intimidated . . . Here is a way for them to convey their message about the question and to feature it at the beginning of the [video]. Something they are proud of that the rest of the class clapped after they saw it. It really brings them into the class and allows their ideas to be viewed and valued.

An enthusiastic Special Education teacher told us how much using computers had changed her teaching. "From the first year of using the computer maybe to retype rough drafts or essays to . . . working on the Internet to actually having students in there for one, two, three days . . . and just letting them go to town."

Of the 13 teachers who said that their teaching had changed, most referred to how they changed their preparation for teaching and how they used computers as another tool to teach. Only four said that they had modified their daily practices in major ways. These four said that they now organized their classes differently, lectured less, relied more on securing information from sources other than the textbook, gave students more independence, and acted more like a coach than a performer on stage. In short, they said that in using technology they had become more student-centered in their teaching; they had made fundamental changes in their pedagogy.

When we shadowed teachers and students, however, we saw what classroom researchers have seen for decades. All but a few of the 35 different teachers (in both schools) used a familiar repertoire of instructional approaches. These routinely lectured, orchestrated a group discussion, reviewed homework, worked on assignments, and occasionally used overhead projectors and videos. From surveying teachers and shadowing students we found that in some classes students gave reports, worked in small groups, or, in the media center, completed projects. For the most part, teacher-centered instruction was the norm, even in computer-based classes.

What we saw among the teachers in these classrooms is consistent with the literature on how most high school teachers teach academic subjects. Seymour Sarason, John Goodlad, Susan Rosenholtz, David Cohen, and many others have documented "the behavioral regularities" (Sarason's phrase) of "frontal teaching" (Goodlad's phrase). Moreover, high school students' observations of their teachers' classroom methods in math, science, U.S. history, and writing support researchers' conclusions regarding widespread practices: teachers lecture, and students listen, read textbooks, and complete individual exercises presented in workbooks or photocopies.[25]

Some champions of computers for classroom instruction have argued that these technologies would eventually be integrated into teachers' repertoires and transform these familiar textbound practices into more intellectually demanding, ambitious instructional practices. Except for the four teachers whom we identified above, we saw little evidence of more student-centered instruction.[26]

These four teachers said that using technologies in their classroom not only had helped them prepare for classes but also had helped make their classrooms more student-centered. What we don't know is whether these changes occurred as a result of the technologies they used or emerged as part of a gradual shift in their beliefs about teaching, in which computers supplied a vehicle for making changes they had already decided upon.

Although the evidence of teaching practices that we have is partial and located at only one point in time, we can draw upon other reports of high school teaching to help answer this question. From our research in the two schools, these incremental changes in how teachers prepare for their classroom lessons have occurred as a consequence of greatly enhanced accessibility to new technologies (especially computers). We can also say that few fundamental changes in the dominant mode of teacher-centered instruction have occurred, except for the four teachers we have mentioned. If anything, what we observed and were told by students suggested strongly that occasional to serious use of computers in their classes had marginal or no impact on routine teaching practices. In other words, most teachers had adapted an innovation to fit their customary practices, not to revolutionize them. Most teachers who adopt technologies such as overhead projectors, VCRs, instructional television, laser disk players, and computers tailor the use of these machines to fit the familiar practices of teacher-centered instruction.[27]

To our first question—to what degree did the national patterns of infrequent and limited teacher use of computers emerge at the two high schools—the answer is: pretty much the same pattern. Despite abundant access to information technologies in both high schools, and contrary to the expectations of promoters, teachers made infrequent and limited teacher use of computers in classrooms. The answer to the second question—to what degree did teachers who used computers in their classrooms typically maintain existing teaching practices—the answer is that teachers who did use computers in their classrooms largely continued their customary practice, again contrary to promoters' expectations. Why, then, does a school's high access yield limited use? Why do teachers adapt new technologies to merely sustain old practices?[28]

The data we gathered from both schools confirm at least two of the reasons commonly offered. One reason often given by teachers and administrators in national data is the lack of time available for teachers to find relevant software, judge its worth, and try out the products in classrooms. This explanation also came up repeatedly in our interviews with teachers and administrators. Nationally and in our case studies, teachers also frequently mentioned that training in relevant software and applications was seldom offered at the times that they needed them. Although many opportunities to learn general computer skills were available in the school district and on-site, teachers felt that the generic training available was often irrelevant to their specific and immediate needs.

The reasons teachers gave us concerning their lack of time and customized training explain only a small part of the unexpected outcomes. There are other explanations, which I will explore in Chapter 5. Three reasons frequently given for the low use of technology and the durability of teacher-centered instruction was not supported by the evidence we compiled, however. Neither the age, experience, nor gender of teachers was a significant factor in our data. We found little difference in computer use between veteran and novice teachers, between those with and those without previous technological experience, or between men and women. Furthermore, we did not find technophobia to be a roadblock. Teachers at both schools called for more and better technology, were avid home users, and believed in the future ubiquity of computers in society.[29]

Next I turn to computer use in higher education, where a super-abundance of information technologies exist. The next chapter is a case study of the intellectual capital of Silicon Valley—Stanford University.

4

NEW TECHNOLOGIES IN OLD UNIVERSITIES

In the late 1960s aggressive administrators at Stanford University secured federal funds to build a multimillion dollar facility called the Stanford Center for Research, Development, and Teaching (SCRDT). A fully furnished television studio with "state-of-the-art" (as the favorite phrase of admirers described it then) cameras, videotape recorders, and monitors occupied the main floor, but the star in the crown of the new building was the Large-Group Instruction room (LGI). This amphitheater-shaped room could hold 160 people. Ten continuous half-circle rows, each row a tad higher than the one below it, could seat from 9 to 28 students, depending on whether the row was at floor level or toward the higher end of the room. At most of the individual seats—or stations, as they were called—was a small punch-button pad called the "student responder." The responder contained the numbers 1–10 and letters Y, N, and O. All of the stations looked down on a small stage with a lectern, a massive pull-down screen, and two large TV monitors suspended from the ceiling above the stage. At the very top of the amphitheater was a glass-enclosed technician's station where an aide could assist the professor with amplification of sound, simultaneous interpretation of various languages, slide or film presentation, and overhead projection of data.

The student responder came into play during lectures. In answer to the professor's questions such as "How many follow the main idea I just described?" "Am I going too quickly over these points?" students pressed "yes," "no," or particular numbers. The data went directly to a mainframe computer, where the students' responses were immediately compiled and displayed at a console on the professor's lectern. The lecturer was then able to adjust the pace and content of the presentation, based on feedback from this advanced interactive technology.

By 1972 when I came to SCRDT as a graduate student, the LGI was being used as a large lecture hall for classes from departments throughout the university. The now-disconnected punch-button pads were toys that students fiddled with during boring lectures. The pull-down screen was used for overheads and occasional films. No technician occupied the dark booth at the rear of the amphitheater. The television studio was still being used by some students and an occasional professor to tape class activities, but the fixed-position cameras purchased in the late 1960s were obsolete and beyond repair.

In 1981, when I returned to Stanford to teach, the SCRDT had been renamed the Center for Educational Research at Stanford (CERAS). None of the original equipment or technology (except the sound system and simultaneous translation) was used by either students or professors. The student responders were still there but had become a harmless anachronism that an occasional professor could cite as an example of a passing technological fad. In 2001 this fully inoperational archeological slice of a technological past is still there—in use as a regular lecture hall not all that different from lecture halls of previous centuries.

When I inquired about the center's swift decay in conversations with staff and veteran faculty who had been around at the time, I was told that few professors had been involved in the design of the building or the LGI. As a result, only 2 of 35 professors in the School of Education had ever used the machinery back when it was operational. Programmers and other technicians were initially hired for faculty support, but in a short time, as federal funds decreased, the support staff was let go. Moreover, the equipment often broke down, and newer machines came on the market that were far better than the original ones purchased by CERAS administrators.[1]

Of course, in the late 1960s many universities shared Stanford's enthusiasm for improving education through technology. And in the decades since, that enthusiasm has not faltered. In the early 1980s, announcements of another "revolution" in teaching and learning swept across American college and university campuses, and university presidents have made major expenditures for new information technologies ever since.

Consider the following items.

- *"How To Hold 250 Undergraduates in the Palm of Your Hand:* Whether you're teaching a hall full of freshmen or a handful of graduate students, nothing makes your lectures more compelling or memorable than creating and delivering them with an Apple Macintosh personal computer." Ad for Macintosh, 1993.[2]
- *"Studio Classrooms: Rensselaer Uses Computers to Replace Large Lectures in Introductory Courses:* A typical two-hour session in studio physics . . . starts with a review of readings and exercises that students have done on their own. The classes (of 50–60) then progress to an experiment that might involve a motion detector attached to a computer to measure the velocity of a falling

golf ball. The session often ends with a 'mini-lecture,' in which the professor summarizes what the students have learned and assigns homework. 'In the studio setting, there's so much more going on in their heads. Instead of four hours of listening and watching, there's four hours of thinking and doing,' says Professor of Mathematics Joseph Ecker who has taught studio calculus."[3]

- "CEO of Cisco Systems, manufacturer of routers that run the Internet, John Chambers predicted that if universities moved too slowly in integrating the Web into their curricula and pedagogy, many students, especially those in telecommunication and computer science fields, 'will go to schools online.'"[4]

- Professor Jerry Porras at Stanford's Graduate School of Business: "I think the day of standing up and being a brilliant lecturer is gone . . . Faculty members will need to combine their brilliant lecturing with the ability to access an interactive database that can speak directly to students' questions. We had better face this, because as an industry [sic] we will no longer be viable over the next 10 to 20 years, if that long."[5]

None of these items would have surprised James Stukel, president of the University of Illinois. He called the Internet and the technology supporting it "the third modern revolution in higher education," after the land-grant movement in the late nineteenth century and the community college upsurge in the early twentieth century. Two veteran observers of higher education had made a similar prediction, reflecting the sturdy optimism about new technologies but also warning higher education leaders what would happen were universities too slow to change. "Information technology (IT) will change teaching and learning profoundly, no matter what the response of traditional higher education institutions . . . If traditional colleges and universities do not exploit the new technologies, other nontraditional providers of education will be quick to do so."[6]

The success of "digital universities" and distance education in capturing an ever-growing chunk of the adult student market has confirmed the academics' predictions. Also confirming their observations has been the occasional accrediting of "virtual universities," places where the only buildings in sight house administrators and machines. But their optimism may have been misplaced. Had our veteran academics, the CEO of Cisco, the Stanford professor, and the president of the University of Illinois examined what has been occurring in professors' classrooms at selective universities across the country in the 1990s—a boom decade for wiring classrooms and technical support—they would have seen a very different picture.[7]

The outcomes that emerged in preschool and K–12 public schools were matched in higher education: the availability of information technologies in classrooms increased dramatically, yet teachers used them infrequently and altered their conventional forms of teaching very little. In this chapter, I will describe the remarkable access that professors have had to information technologies both at home and on campus; their abundant use of these technologies for their own research, communication with peers and administrators, and preparation for teaching but not for instruction; and the outcomes of these uses, both anticipated and unanticipated.

ACCESS TO NEW TECHNOLOGY

Major bargains struck between corporate vendors and university officials in the early 1980s brought to American campuses an enormous array of state-of-the-art hardware and software. Through deals negotiated with IBM and Apple, thousands of machines and software flowed into administrative suites, student labs, and faculty offices. In the 1990s, heavy capital investments in wiring, hardware upgrades, and technical support gave individual professors an office computer, communication links to labs across campus, wired classrooms, email, Internet access, and technical support staff. In 1994 alone, American colleges and universities spent more than $6 billion for machines, wiring, software, and technical support. Almost $2 billion was spent to support instruction. With more than 15,000,000 students enrolled for 1994, this translates to about $400 per student in overall expenditures for technology and about $115 per student for instructional uses. Five years later, the spending has continued but at a less torrid pace. For the school year 1999–2000, total projected spending for academic computer hardware and software will top $2.7 billion. As in K–12 expenditures, these amounts are small compared to overall funding, but they nonetheless represent sharp increases targeted for particular goals. Moreover, virtually all professors privately invested in a computer at home.[8]

As a result of these substantial increases in access to information technologies, remarkable changes have occurred in how students use computers in dorms, labs, libraries, and elsewhere on wired campuses. Furthermore, most professors conduct their research, produce publications, communicate in their scholarly disciplines, and prepare for teaching through electronic means. Yet when it comes to teaching, few close observers would deny that most professors in colleges and universities are either nonusers or occasional users of computer technology in the classroom.[9]

CLASSROOM USE OF COMPUTERS

Academics tend not to be technophobes. At home and in the office they use computers to write, analyze data, communicate with colleagues, and draft syllabi and other materials for courses. Nor are professors resistant to learning new machines and software applications. Personal accounts and surveys report again and again that most academics are enthusiastic about the usefulness of computers and other technologies for routine tasks in laboratories and lecture halls.

Furthermore, adventurous faculty on campus after campus have designed software for particular topics in their discipline; they have adapted existing applications to classes that they teach; they have experimented with email, Web-based classes, and other forms of distance learning; they have been the first to sign up for "studio" classrooms at Rensselaer, teaching/learning theaters at the University of Maryland (College Park), and the Flexible Class-Lab at Stanford. But these pioneers are a tiny minority. One estimate put this small band of early adopters at less than 5 percent of the faculty on any given campus. Getting mainstream faculty on board, or, more to the point, persuading "laggards" to become serious users is much more difficult.[10]

Computers and other new technologies have had little tangible effect on either classroom teaching or learning—certainly nothing comparable to the major pedagogical changes that occurred in the decades bridging the turn of the twentieth century, when labs, seminars, and discussion sections were introduced to supplement lecturing. Still, the lecture has remained central to undergraduate instruction and the seminar to graduate programs. Throughout the 1970s and 1980s, national faculty surveys recorded time and again that lecturing was the prevailing mode of teaching, followed by group discussion. In one national survey, 80 percent of 829 randomly selected professors (representing a 79 percent return of questionnaires) in the physical sciences, life sciences, mathematics, social sciences, and humanities lectured for the entire period, and an additional 9 percent said that they lectured from 15 to 25 minutes.[11] In 1995 and 1998, surveys of teaching methods were sent to 71,000 professors of undergraduate instruction in private and public colleges and universities; there was a 42 percent response. The results are shown in Table 13.

Experiences at Carnegie-Mellon and Brown University during the 1980s and early 1990s underscore the vast and swift changes that occurred in the ease with which professors adopted personal computers for their research, communication, and preparation for teaching. Yet most of these very same professors found computers difficult to apply to their classroom instruction.[12] In these institutions a striking but now-familiar puzzle had emerged. Faculty have unparalleled access to infor-

Table 13. Instructional Methods Used in Most or All Undergraduate Courses

Method	1995–1996	1998–1999
Extensive lecturing	55%	53%
Class discussions	65%	65%
Computer/machine-aided instruction	14%	17%

Sources: Linda Sax, Alexander Astin, William Korn, Shannon Gilmartin, *The American College Teacher: National Norms for the 1998–1999 HERI Faculty Survey* (Los Angeles: Higher Education Research Institute, UCLA, 1999), p. 36; Linda Sax, Alexander Astin, Marisol Avedondo, William Korn, *The American College Teacher: National Norms for the 1995–1996 HERI Faculty Survey* (Los Angeles: Higher Education Research Institute, UCLA, 1996), p. 39.

mation technologies at home and office; they use these machines and software frequently for their research and course preparation. Yet for instruction in their classrooms they use computers infrequently and in limited ways, producing few changes in how they teach and how their students learn. What has become increasingly apparent across the nation is nowhere more so than at Stanford University, an elite private research-driven institution.[13]

STANFORD UNIVERSITY

Although the 125 public and private research universities included in the early 1990s Carnegie classification of Research I and II universities amounted to less than 4 percent of the nation's 3,600 higher education institutions, they enrolled almost 20 percent of all college students. Equally important, since the early twentieth century these few institutions have set the standards for judging other universities, 4- and 2-year colleges, and even secondary schools.[14] They have had a disproportionate influence on curricular and instructional practices in higher education both in the United States and abroad. The establishment of Johns Hopkins University, Clark, and the University of Chicago in the last decade of the nineteenth century, for example, spurred reforms in existing colleges. Curricular reforms at Columbia during World War I or at the University of Chicago in the 1930s or at Harvard in the 1950s attracted the attention of administrators and faculties at hundreds of other less prestigious institutions. Since then, U.S. research-centered universities have been imitated by many nations.[15]

Over a century ago, university presidents set as the gold standard for their institutions the advancement of knowledge through research, especially in the physical and natural sciences. As professors published their scholarship, the upward path to national (and international) prestige for other institutions of higher learning narrowed to this one route: the research-driven university. And copy it they did. In an effort to reproduce an academic culture attractive to research-minded faculty, less-prestigious, status-seeking institutions reduced teaching loads, introduced sabbaticals, and established large graduate schools. The trickle-down influence of the major universities can also be seen in the careers of each new generation of the professoriate, which receives its graduate training in top research universities and then goes on to serve on faculties lower down in the hierarchy. These professors take with them expectations about reduced teaching loads and research support that were fostered in the elite universities.[16]

Stanford university has been considered a research-oriented institution since it joined the Association of American Universities in 1900. In that decade it was ranked as one of the "best" universities in the nation, though in fact it was little more than a strong regional institution on the West Coast. In the 1950s, however, Stanford's Board of Trustees charged its president with establishing the university as a strong national presence rather than merely a regional one.

By the late 1960s Stanford had moved into the first tier of universities as measured by qualifications of faculty and students, size of endowment, and available research funds. By the 1990s, reputational rankings of departments and undergraduate and graduate programs by both popular news magazines and scholarly studies continually placed Stanford in the top five institutions in the country. As a selective Research I university,

Stanford is representative of similar elite institutions, both public and private, in the United States.[17]

At Stanford, as at most other high-status universities, governance is split between administration and faculty, departmental organization is decentralized, and faculty members are granted autonomy to inquire, freedom to teach with available tools, and entrepreneurial discretion in securing research grants. But like its sister institutions, Stanford has faced tensions over how faculty time should be distributed between undergraduate teaching and working on individual research projects, especially given that tenure decisions are so clearly linked to the volume and quality of scholarly publication, not to teaching effectiveness. This conflict of interest—being hired to teach but rewarded for doing research—emerged early in the twentieth century among professors in all of the elite institutions. Discord arose frequently within departments over how much time and which courses faculty should build into the curriculum to ensure that undergraduates were exposed to essential knowledge in the humanities and sciences and still leave sufficient time for professors to specialize in their disciplines.

Stanford and other private and public universities have sought to strike a balance between maintaining stability and encouraging innovation as they negotiated their path through turbulent, unpredictable times. Such a balance has become increasingly difficult to reach in an information-based society in which students expect quality teaching, corporate leaders call for more applied research, public officials seek advice from university experts, and parents want prestigious diplomas to open doors to high-paying jobs for their sons and daughters. Furthermore, all of these constituencies want the newest, fastest, and best technology that money can buy so that professors can teach and students can learn productively. And where better to find the newest of the new technology than in Silicon Valley? The history of Stanford University is deeply entwined with the story of how the once-bucolic Santa Clara valley became a technological Mecca.[18]

ACCESS TO COMPUTING AT STANFORD

Starting in the 1950s, Presidents Wallace Sterling, Richard Lyman, Donald Kennedy, and Gerhard Casper worked hard through periods of growth, recession, and turbulence to enhance the faculty, build modern facilities, and expand the prestige of their institution. They succeeded. With more than 14,000 students taught by almost 1,600 tenure-line faculty deployed in 70 departments and schools across an 8,000-acre campus, Stanford's reputation as a world-class university is firmly grounded. In the move to world-class status, possessing the newest and best technologies in the arts, sciences, and humanities became essential. President Gerhard Casper summed up the reasons, past and present, for harnessing information technologies to the university's mission: "Appropriate use of information resources can increase faculty productivity; help to attract, retain, and engage the brightest students; enrich students' learning experiences and faculty teaching methods. Technology may enhance income opportunities for the University and potentially reduce costs of delivering education." University leadership, from Wallace Sterling to the newly-installed president John Hennessy has forged ahead full speed into the information revolution.[19]

But in doing so, Stanford has incurred steep costs. "Looking ahead," a staff member reported, "we can expect to need a new computer every three years. These computers will assume an increasingly large role in Stanford's research and education. They will cost increasingly large amounts of money." These predictions, made in the first annual report of Stanford's Computation Center, proved prophetic. The year was 1961.[20] During the 1960s and 1970s, top administrators centralized computing at Stanford. Working with mainframe machines, they confined computing largely to the automation of administrative tasks in offices and libraries, with some data analysis and model building in scientific and engineering research. One exception was the federally funded SCRDT described at the beginning of this chapter. With the introduction of the personal computer in the late 1970s, however, a decade of partnerships with vendors who supplied machines to faculty and departments yielded thousands of computers in short-lived ventures.

Administrators prodded department chairs and faculty to use the new technologies for streamlining tasks and doing research and teaching in their offices and classrooms. But because administrators often negotiated the terms of the partnerships with vendors, aggressive departments well endowed with funds got more information technology than timid, less affluent departments. The administrative and academic cultures at Stanford competed for influence over the deployment of the machines and software and how they were to be used. "The most important single lesson administratively about Stanford's use of computers," said a professor who participated enthusiastically in applying technologies to instruction, "is that use is not in any sense organized centrally. It is a blooming chaos of pluralism and I think most faculty very much want it to be that way." This characteristic decentralization played a large role in the rapid adoption of computers by individual professors for use in their research, communication with colleagues, and teaching.[21]

By the mid-1980s, the personal computer had trumped the mainframe for daily academic and administrative uses. Swift changes in the speed and memory of the machines and in software development kept outpacing the ability of university task forces to set policy. Still, Stanford administrators and faculty who had enlisted in the information revolution continued to conceive programs aimed at encouraging professors to use computers in their courses.

One such program launched in 1984 was the jointly funded University/IBM/Apple Faculty Author Development program (with the unfortunate but wholly prescient acronym FAD). According to one administrator, the purpose was to "build a critical mass of faculty who would use computers for teaching, who were knowledgeable enough to decide how useful computers could be instead of having [administrative units] push computers on the faculty."[22]

The 18 professors from Humanities and Sciences (H&S) who volunteered (out of about 450 faculty in H&S at the time) received hardware and expert help from technical support staff to develop courseware for their classes. But few other professors used the courseware developed by these pioneers. Toward the end of the decade it was clear to most faculty and administrators that FAD and other incentive-based programs geared to enlist faculty in using computers for classroom instruction had failed to entice most professors. As one administrator said in 1987, "The crime of it is computers aren't used more [by the faculty], in spite of all the money spent on [technology]."[23]

Not to be discouraged, administrators took the basic infrastructure for technology that had been built in the 1980s and spent more to enhance that foundation. Throughout the 1990s, administrators invested university funds in laying down miles of fiberoptic cables to offices, networking the campus, providing computer clusters in libraries and in residence halls, building elaborate computer labs for professors and their classes, and ensuring that faculty had on-site specialists in departments and schools to assist them in using information technology for both their research and teaching.

By 2000 the Leland system of computers and networks was serving Stanford students, faculty, and staff with email, Web resources, and other services, while the Forsythe system served instructional, research, and interactive computing. Scattered across campus are clusters of machines (with more than 350 high-powered personal computers and workstations) available to students in libraries, the student union, and engineering buildings. All undergraduate residence halls and certain graduate halls have computer clusters with, again, more than 350 computers staffed by coordinators and technicians. Servers provide file sharing, printing, Internet access, and database and groupware services for computer labs and clusters in individual schools such as the Graduate School of Business, School of Medicine, Humanities and Sciences, School of Earth Sciences, Education, Law, and School of Engineering.

Moreover, the administration has wired more than 60 classrooms across campus with video and computer display and network connections. Each classroom contains a color LCD video/data projector, VCR, and amplified sound system with a "smart panel" that controls power and volume controls. Of the 60 plus classrooms, three in the main undergraduate library are widely used by faculty who bring their classes of up to 40 students there.[24]

In response to faculty requests for help throughout the decade, a constant stream of faculty workshops on topics from designing Web pages to developing courseware have been advertised each year. University-funded computer specialists have been assigned to particular schools to be on-site sources of individual help to faculty beyond the specific technical support staff that departments and schools have funded out of their regular budgets.[25]

By the late 1990s, then, Stanford students and faculty had abundant and easy access to information technologies in residences, schools, departments, offices, labs, and libraries. From registering for courses on-line to doing research on the Web to entering chat rooms to renewing library books, Stanford students' lives are perfused with electronic technology. Undergraduates reported in a 1994 survey that they used computers 11 hours a week, and graduate students averaged more than 18 hours of computer use a week. Furthermore, both students and faculty had their own machines. In 1996, for example, 3 out of 4 students owned a personal computer. By 2000, 95 percent had their own machines, which allowed them to connect to Stanford networks in their rooms. The Law School now requires entering students to own laptops.

As early as 1989, nine out of ten faculty in the School of Humanities and Sciences used some form of computing in their work. A similar number had at least one computer at home. In 1999 virtually all professors had computers at their offices and homes, and most had more than two machines available to them. According to a 1997 survey, 61 percent of the faculty owned a laptop in addition to a networked desktop computer or workstation. Computers have become as pervasive on and off the Stanford campus as telephones, televisions, and microwave ovens. In light of this massive investment in new technologies, how have Stanford faculty used computers inside classrooms?[26]

How Stanford Professors Teach

Since the 1960s, the normal professorial teaching load has been 4 to 6 hours a week (or 4 courses taught over 3 quarters of a 4-quarter academic year), down from a class load of 8 to 12 hours a week and 6 to 8 courses that faculty taught in the early 1900s. Evidence of how Stanford professors taught for those 4 to 6 hours a week is difficult to come by, because few campus-wide faculty surveys of teaching practices were administered before the 1990s. There were, however, partial surveys of professorial teaching, reports, and even questionnaires that seniors completed before leaving the university. Although such fragments are hardly compelling evidence of how professors taught, they do offer a glimpse of the dominant teaching practices.[27]

In 1968 graduating seniors reported in a questionnaire that two-thirds to four-fifths of all their classes in engineering, science, social science, and humanities were either large lectures or medium-sized lectures with discussion. Their experiences with seminars ranged from a low of 9 percent in the sciences to a high of 33 percent in the humanities. Seniors also reported that some courses included independent work, ranging from 11 percent in engineering to 24 percent in sciences.[28]

In 1994, as part of a presidential-appointed panel, the Commission on Undergraduate Education (CUE) authorized a survey that went out to 750 professors who taught undergraduates. One question asked whether professors used "non-traditional modes of teaching." Professors marked either yes or no. The highest number of yes votes went for student presentations (57 percent), followed by small group work (39 percent) and case studies (26 percent). Highest percentages of no votes went to in-class writing (92), brainstorming (90), role playing (86), debates (84), simulations (84), and case studies (74). The results imply strongly that traditional teaching approaches such as lecturing were staples in most professors' instructional repertoires.[29]

In 1995, in a survey of 116 professors across the campus, Nira Hativa found that 78 percent "almost always" lectured and answered student questions during or after the lecture. Two-thirds "almost always" lectured and then held separate discussion groups under the guidance of teaching assistants or the professor himself or herself. Just under 30 percent taught "almost always" by "developing topics through questioning the students (Socratic method)."[30]

In 1996 President Casper announced a $15 million initiative to strengthen undergraduate teaching by adding faculty positions. Recognizing that large lecture courses for undergraduates are the norm, Casper underscored the importance of first- and second-year students having direct contact in seminars with professors rather than graduate students. Subsequently, freshman and sophomore seminars have been established where faculty teach small groups of undergraduates (who must apply for the limited slots).[31]

In 1997 a student newspaper ran an editorial that said "Professors' reliance on TAs [teaching assistants] has grown to scandalous proportions." Calling the widespread use of TAs for introductory courses a "stealth scandal," the *Stanford Daily* said that the "use and abuse of graduate students has gone too far.

The discussion section—which started out as a venue for students to ask questions to their more knowledgeable peers—has metamorphosed into the core of far too many lecture courses."[32] Although the evidence is admittedly circumstantial, the impression that lecturing is the dominant form of undergraduate teaching persists. But "dominant" in this instance does not mean it is the only form of teaching, nor that the lecture approach will continue to prevail.

Some professors, for example, reported using different forms of teaching (case studies, project-based teaching, problem-based learning) within various departments and schools across campus. In the Business and Law schools, many faculty use the case method. In the School of Education, Professor Ed Bridges created an entire program for master's students who seek to become school principals that is anchored in problem-based, collaborative learning in small groups. The School of Engineering has paid explicit attention to the quality of teaching since the 1950s.[33]

The History Department and the preclinical program in the School of Medicine (SUSM), both dating back to Stanford's founding, offer brief snapshots of teaching practices in two very different parts of the university.[34] By 1990, lecturing absorbed at least one-half to two-thirds of teaching duties in SUSM's preclinical courses and in the Department of History, with the remainder of formal instructional time spent in seminars, laboratory work, discussion sections, and directed research with individuals and small groups of students. With some slight variation by departments, this pattern in teaching permeates the rest of the campus and is similar to other American universities.

Over the century in SUSM and in the Department of History, small-group teaching and students' independent work slowly spread from its original home in graduate school (for early twentieth-century doctoral students and medical students in the clinical phase of their work) to the final two years of an undergraduate's career and initial preclinical courses for entering medical students. Such changes have lessened the impersonality of lecturing to hundreds of students in cavernous auditoriums. Yet even with the mild decrease in lecturing over the century and the increase in small-group teaching, the lecture still dominates preclinical instruction in SUSM and undergraduate history courses.[35]

For the rest of the university in the 1990s, this teaching repertoire remained steadfast. Two surveys revealed sharply that few faculty members use nontraditional methods (information technologies, case studies, simulations), and those who do are a tiny fraction of the Stanford professoriate, a pattern generally applicable to American universities.[36]

With so much instructional time still devoted to the lecture, it is not surprising that lecturing has become equated with teaching. What forged the link even tighter were the faculty's core beliefs about the role of subject matter in teaching. Many History and SUSM faculty continue to believe that the central purpose of teaching is to transmit their discipline's accumulated knowledge to students. According to faculty, undergraduates must gain an elementary grasp of the field before advancing to higher levels of disciplinary inquiry. Hence the dominant teaching role is that of content-disseminator. Because it is more efficient to convey subject matter and the essentials of a discipline to large groups than to small ones, the lecture prevails and the role of professor as platform performer links to the role of disseminator of content. Pedagogy is no more than a delivering system for clear and coherent knowledge. Those who know can teach.[37]

Yet some faculty have held (and continue to hold) counter-beliefs. Teaching for student understanding rather than factual coverage has motivated many professors to practice their craft differently from their colleagues. Such beliefs drive some professors to find out how students learn, figure out the issues that confound novices in a field, and teach content in ways that unravel what students find difficult.

In teaching calculus to undergraduates, for example, some math professors have restructured their courses to teach the subject through problems that are connected to the students' lives. To teach approximations, a professor might ask students to graph the rising temperature of a yam put into a hot oven and estimate the time at which the temperature of the yam would be 150 degrees. Such professors probe and guide students in learning conceptual structures of a discipline; they seek to help students learn how to think as mathematicians, historians, or medical clinicians.[38] In SUSM, a new faculty-designed preclinical course, "Preparation for Clinical Medicine," begins with beliefs that students could learn essential clinical knowledge and skills in small groups with preceptors, rather than lecturers, by concentrating on common problems faced by practitioners.[39]

Some faculty hold prevailing and counter-beliefs about pedagogy simultaneously, enacting each in particular settings. Consider the historians David Potter, who taught in the 1960s and early 1970s, and David Kennedy, who has taught since the late 1960s. Both have taught lecture courses and seminars. Their students have described the professors as engaging platform performers who, in advanced seminars, use analogies and metaphors to represent complex ideas while prodding individual students to think like historians.[40]

USE OF COMPUTERS FOR INSTRUCTION

Here, then, is a partial picture of how most Stanford professors have taught. Against such a background, faculty use of new technologies to improve teaching and learning can be assessed.

One way of finding out about classroom use of computers is to tap the periodic surveys that have been done by doctoral students, faculty, and administrators over the years. Of course, surveys are essentially self-reports and so are prone to inflation and selective memory. Moreover, response rates from faculty surveys tend to be low. Unfortunately, despite these weaknesses, there is little else to cite beyond scattered anecdotes by techno-enthusiasts and techno-skeptics. The surveys do cover the important decades at Stanford after major investments were made in wiring and in purchasing personal computers, after task force reports on the direction of computing had been published, and after faculty incentive projects had been initiated.

In the mid-1980s, one study of 125 Stanford professors found the following:

- 80 percent of professors used computers to prepare lectures, handouts, and exams.
- About 25 percent of professors required students to write their papers on a computer or analyze a database.
- Only 13 professors (10 percent) had actually integrated the computer into their routine classroom practices.[41]

In 1989 a survey sent to more than 660 faculty in Humanities and Sciences found that:

- 94 percent of professors used computers for their research, class preparation, and writing.
- 80 percent of faculty used computers to prepare handouts.
- 72 percent used them to design exams.
- 62 percent used them to prepare lectures.
- 13 percent of professors used computers for demonstrations in the classroom.
- 20 percent used them for computer exercises.
- 10 percent actually used subject-related software.[42]

Another faculty survey in 1994 found even less classroom use of technologies. This survey, which went out to 750 professors who taught undergraduates, showed that:

- 59 percent of the professors never used computers in their classrooms.
- 19 percent used computers occasionally.
- 8 percent used computers often (the remaining responses were not usable).
- 2 out of 3 professors responding to this survey said that the lack of time to develop relevant software for their courses was a strong factor in their nonuse.
- 45 percent said that they had no time to learn about classroom uses of computers.
- 70–90 percent of the faculty responded that they had not used any of the consultants available in five university centers.[43]

In 1997 another faculty survey was sent to 750 professors across campus. The results for this unpublished survey mirror earlier ones. To the question "What technologies do you use in the classroom, and how frequently do you use them?" the percentage of faculty that responded "Never" was:

- "computer at instructor station": 62%
- "computers at student stations": 85%
- "LCD Panel": 83%
- "Internet/Web Connection": 80%

The 1989 and 1997 questionnaires show that the two machines faculty used most often (from occasionally to frequently) were the overhead projector and the VCR.[44]

Several themes ran through these surveys. Repeatedly, faculty indicated a strong interest, even enthusiasm, for using new technologies but cited as reasons for not making any headway their lack of time to learn how to use computers well and to develop software. Faculty were reluctant to take valuable time away from research, teaching, writing, securing grants, committee work, and other important tasks. A consistent concern expressed was not having reliable, accessible, and continuing support from technical staff when problems arose.[45]

For technologically assertive administrators and faculty, these figures may offer a skewed picture of what they see happening in departments and schools across campus. They might well point to the three specially equipped classrooms located in the main undergraduate library, to which faculty bring full classes periodically or for the entire quarter to teach their courses. I have secured lists of the professors who have used two of the three classrooms. Fragmentary as such data are, the lists offer a broader picture of faculty use, albeit one that is partial, but that at least goes beyond anecdotes and survey responses.[46]

The Flexible Class-Lab seats 25 students and contains 20 PowerBook laptop computers, network connections, computer and video projection, scanning equipment, and—most important for many faculty who want movable furniture for small group work and seminar discussion—lightweight tables, office chairs, and beanbags. For the Flexible Class-Lab I have data from 1996, when the classroom became available, through 1999.

Room 143 can accommodate 45 students. It has the latest data and video projection equipment that lets faculty direct images from different computers onto a large screen. The room also contains a VCR and laser disk player. Faculty bring their classes here to demonstrate software, to lecture, and to lead discussions. For Room 143, I have data from January 1998 through October 1999.

Room 260 is a computer classroom that has 20 student stations equipped with iMacs connected to a file server in the room and to the Internet. A color LCD projector allows professors to project computer or video images onto a large screen. A laser printer and color scanner are also in the room. No data on past use are available for this classroom.

For room 143 and the Flexible Class-Lab, 47 faculty (13 tenured professors, 2 tenure-line, and 27 lecturers) used the two classrooms over three academic years.[47] These faculty, who taught 87 courses, were drawn from the departments of English (12, mostly Writing and Critical Thinking courses), Education (7), Foreign Languages (7), Culture, Ideas, and Values (4), Human Biology (4), Engineering (4), Computer Science (2), Law (2), Anthropology (1), History (1), Classics (1), Economics (1), and Sociology (1). Of the 47 professors, 11 (23 percent) accounted for 46 of the 87 courses (53 percent) that were taught.

Among the pioneering faculty, then, about one-quarter taught over half of the courses that met in the two classrooms over a three-year period.[48] These adventurous professors and lecturers were drawn from the ranks of both senior and junior, male and female, faculty. The familiar claims that older, experienced faculty and men rather than women tend to be the pioneers and serious users of computer technology find no basis in these data.

These data show that over the last two decades a small portion of the 1,600 tenure-line faculty members have been very serious about using new technologies in their daily teaching practice in the classroom. These few professors are the subjects of the many positive stories that have appeared over the years in campus publications and in general newspapers and magazines extolling the magic of computers in classrooms. Media portrayals of these early adopters leave the impression that mainstream faculty members engage the technology in the same spirit, if not with quite the same proficiency, that their noted colleagues do. The surveys and classroom data, however, suggest that most academics have yet to seriously pursue the use of computers for instruction.[49]

Since the late 1970s, these early adopters have pioneered software for their courses and have embraced technological improvements to personal computers as they were developed. For example, members of the President's Commission on Technology in Teaching and Learning (CTTL), appointed by Gerhard Casper in 1994, have been ardent supporters of frequent and imaginative uses of these powerful technologies for improving teaching and learning. Some entrepreneurial academics were part of the FAD initiative in the early 1980s and have emerged as technological leaders in the Stanford community in the 1990s. These professors have created multimedia Web pages, have made their courses available on the Internet, and have proven to be quite at home in electronically enhanced classrooms. Other faculty, tired of teaching in traditional ways, have yearned for opportunities to try out some of these new media for classroom instruction.

Consider Lecturer Marjorie Ford's course "Writing and Critical Thinking." The class met in the Flex-Class Lab to explore methods of using technology to support writing. Students developed Web pages, critiqued one another's work, integrated pictures into the writing process, and in general collaborated more than one customarily does in writing classes. "I always thought," Ford said, "that in a writing class the students ought to be writing more. That is what's happening in the Flex Lab. The room invites you to work with students, not just lecture at them."[50]

Associate Professor Yvonne Yarbro-Bejarano of the Spanish and Portuguese Department worked with the Academic Software Development group to create *Chicana Art*, a multimedia database of works by various Mexican-American artists. The slides were electronically scanned and linked to what the artists have said, their biographies, and lists of references. "I used to be very centered in print, and I would teach writing and literature," she said, but "now I can't consider just looking at text anymore. I feel that we've barely scratched the surface."[51]

Professor of Electrical Engineering Stephen Boyd often uses computer simulations to predict outcomes in circuits, displaying the results in his class for students to discuss. In labs where there are signal generators, oscilloscopes, and other instrumentation, he has his students actually build circuits to check out their predictions. The soft-lab (computer simulations) and hard-lab (building circuits) approaches that Boyd uses employ different technologies. In addition, Boyd makes his course notes available on the Web the day before class. He has learned that instructors in other universities are using his notes in their own classrooms.[52]

English Professor Larry Friedlander entered the world of instructional computing in 1984 when he developed a computer software program through FAD that would help students interpret Shakespeare's plays. *TheaterGame* permits students to stage via the computer their own interpretations of a play. He also authored *Paris/Theater,* a program that contains maps of Paris and other sources between the twelfth century and the present. Friedlander wanted to find "ways in which literary classes could get some notion of the theatrical and the real-life experiences of literature that are hard to conceptualize in large lecture classes."[53]

These four faculty members are at the level of appropriation and invention in integrating computers into their teaching. Such a high level of integration makes student learning different from the familiar fare offered in most academic classes. How many other professors who use computers in their courses can match these levels of integration I do not know conclusively. However, I would estimate no more than 1 to 2 percent of the entire faculty.

When considering these various examples and data, one should keep a few distinctions in mind as a way of making sense of both numbers and anecdotes. First, a clear separation has to be made between faculty using computers to *prepare for* instruction and faculty actually using computers *for* instruction. There is no question that the former use is pervasive: professors throughout the university use computers to prepare handouts, they use the Internet for information that can be accessed before or after class, and they use email listservers so that students can respond to one another before and after class. However, the percentage of faculty using computers during instruction itself is very low.[54]

Second, survey data may mislead because results mask the variation in departmental and school use across the university.[55] At the Law School, students use laptops for email, research, Internet searches, word processing, note-taking, and even exam-taking. Moreover, two professors teach courses on cyberspace and the law, biotechnology, technology as a business asset, and intellectual property rights vis-à-vis electronic publication. One of the two used a specially equipped classroom for one of these courses. Whether most law school professors were serious, occasional, or nonusers of technology for instruction I cannot determine.[56]

In the School of Medicine, a wide array of technological resources is available to faculty and students in the main medical school building, which houses six lecture classrooms equipped with multimedia technology. The Fleischmann Laboratories are located on the second floor of the Alway Building. Each of the six laboratories is equipped with a computer that is used to access software programs supporting laboratory-based courses. The laboratories are also used for elective courses, conferences, and seminars. The Fleischmann Learning and Resource Center (FLRC) is adjacent to the laboratories, providing students and faculty with a wide variety of video and electronic resources, including videotapes of all lectures. Portable classrooms contain three examination rooms and six small classrooms used for small-group discussions.[57]

In the late 1970s, when the Department of Anatomy within the medical school came under extensive attack from both students and faculty for the low quality of teaching, the administration and faculty of the School of Medicine acted. Within five years, the department had been downsized to a division, new faculty had been hired who had reputations for teaching rather than research, and interactive software to teach basic anatomy courses became a standard part of the curriculum.[58]

By the early 1990s, the School of Medicine administration and faculty had developed an in-house capability for producing software to be used by professors in both the preclinical and clinical curricula. Stanford University Medical Media and Information Technologies (SUMMIT) has created, in collaboration with enthusiastic faculty, "Anatomy Lesson," "BrainStorm," "Microbe," "ShortRounds," and other interactive software that students use in actual courses taught in the School of Medicine. SUMMIT also helped a group of faculty develop materials for a new preclinical course called "Preparation for Clinical Medicine" which blends problem-based learning, multiple-station exercises, faculty-student collaboration, and small group work.[59]

Administrators and faculty in other schools and departments such as the Graduate School of Business and the School of Engineering have moved aggressively into capturing technological resources and applying them to curriculum, teaching, and learning. But many other departments and schools, in the eyes of techno-enthusiasts on campus, have lagged behind and done little to alter prevailing ways of teaching and learning through greater instructional use of computers in classrooms. Stanford Online is an exception. As a distance-learning operation in various incarnations since the late 1960s, Stanford Online offers courses and one degree to corporations in the Bay area, the nation, and internationally. It is a major venture that has faculty teaching students through courses that they would ordinarily give in university buildings. Centered in the sciences, technology, and engineering, this distance-learning program raises much revenue for the university.[60]

The stories, sign-up lists, and survey results from Stanford still leave the strong, clear impression that most faculty are serious users of new technologies for their research, writing, and classroom preparation but infrequent and limited users of the same technologies in their daily teaching. What is also very obvious is that the substantial investment in computers, wired residence halls, and computer labs scattered across the campus have expanded student opportunities to learn outside of formal classroom instruction.

I have concluded, then, that dominant teaching practices remained largely constant in the years of greatest penetration of new technologies. Lecturing still absorbs more than half to two thirds of various departments' teaching practices, especially for undergraduates. Seminars, an innovation that was introduced at the turn of the last century, have become integral to graduate instruction and have penetrated the last two years of undergraduate coursework. These traditional forms of teaching seem to have been relatively untouched by the enormous investment in technologies that the university has made since the 1960s. That individual professors in various departments and schools turned to the case-study method, project-based teaching, problem-based learning, and other innovative approaches, using computer simulations and applications, goes without saying. That such faculty constituted a tiny minority of the entire faculty is just as clear.

So outcomes similar to those that appeared in the early childhood sites and the two high schools also emerge at Stanford University. Both at home and at school, Stanford students and faculty have stunning access to technological riches. Both professors and students use the machines and software extensively to research, write, communicate, and prepare for courses. Yet for direct classroom instruction there is little use of these new technologies.

A second finding is that the primary reason given by university boards of trustees and presidents for investing money and time in an expensive technological infrastructure over the decades is to "revolutionize" teaching and learning. As the evidence suggests, however, there has been, at best, modest to little impact on the teaching strategies commonly used. As to whether student learning has been altered, there is more evidence of frequent use of computers in dorms, labs, libraries, and elsewhere on campus for both class work, research, and personal communication than in K–12.

Like Silicon Valley teachers in preschools, kindergartens, and high schools, Stanford professors are hardly technophobes or skeptics resistant to using technology outside of their classrooms. Why, then, in the heartland of high-tech innovation, where beliefs in technological progress run strong and equipment is abundant, has there been so little use of the new machines and software inside classrooms and so little change in existing teaching practices? I attempt to answer this question in the next chapter.

5

MAKING SENSE OF UNEXPECTED OUTCOMES

In mid-nineteenth century California, entrepreneurs imported the blue gum eucalyptus from Australia, a fast-growing tree needing little water that could in a few years' time reforest treeless areas. The wood would be used for railroad ties, houses, and furniture.

However, as it turned out, the wood would often split or curve while being cut for logs. And it contained so many cracks that nails or spikes would not hold, making it unusable for homebuilding or rail ties. So the tall, fast-growing trees ended up as wind breaks in rural areas, but the fragrant leaves, nut-like seeds, and peeling bark created mounds of litter; even worse, during dry months the canopy often ignited, causing fires to sweep through elegant residential areas and threaten hillside homes.[1]

Such unintended outcomes—sometimes called "revenge effects"—happen all the time. A miracle vaccine to prevent polio in children turned out to have been contaminated with a monkey virus that caused a lethal cancer. The vacuum cleaner and washing machine were intended to improve the standard of living of middle-class housewives. But as it turned out, these conveniences saved little time, because now women who previously had hired housemaids and sent their dirty clothes to a commercial laundry felt obliged to clean their houses by themselves and do their wash at home.[2]

As long as there have been political and business elites, academics, planners, and ordinary reformers determined to solve societal problems, there have been, in Robert Merton's phrase, "unanticipated consequences." Whether the unintended outcomes were the result of ignorance, error, vested interest, or some mix of these mattered little. Few of the problemsolvers who design the solutions are still around by the time their unanticipated consequences must be addressed.[3]

Even though Merton reminded his readers that unforeseen consequences are not necessarily undesirable, the examples usually cited to illustrate the phrase are mostly negative. But the things we don't foresee are just as likely to be positive as negative. For example, when compulsory attendance laws required parents to enroll their children in public schools in the nineteenth century, coed schooling opened job opportunities for young women that previously had been closed.[4]

In answering the questions that guided this study, I found some outcomes that promoters intended, and some that were clearly unintended.

In the area of access to computers:

- *Expected finding:* Students and teachers had access to computers and related technologies available in both their homes and their schools.[5]
- *Unexpected finding:* Students and teachers showed little evidence of technophobia or resistance to using information technologies.

As for the way computers were used in schools:

- *Expected finding:* Those teachers who used computers at home, office, and school said that they communicated much more with colleagues, parents, and students than they had previously; they completed administrative tasks connected to teaching more efficiently (calculating student grades, writing notes to parents, compiling attendance reports, and so on); and they prepared for teaching with more depth and breadth in creating materials for student handouts and Internet searches.

- *Unexpected finding:* Less than 10 percent of teachers who used computers in their classrooms were serious users (defined as using computers in class at least once week); between 20 and 30 percent were occasional to rare users (once a month); well over half of the teachers were nonusers.[6]

- *Unexpected finding:* In classrooms of serious and occasional users, most students' use of computers was peripheral to their primary instructional tasks. Students used computers in schools to complete assignments, play games, explore CD-ROMS to find information, and conduct Internet searches. Only on rare occasions did student computer use become of primary importance, as in participating in on-line curriculum and creating multimedia projects.

- *Unexpected finding:* Less than 5 percent of high school students had intense "tech-heavy" experiences. These occurred mostly in nonacademic subjects or when students served as part of the school's technical support system.

- *Unexpected finding:* Less than 5 percent of teachers integrated computer technology into their regular curricular and instructional routines.

These findings about access and use led to unexpected outcomes for teaching and learning:

- *Unexpected outcome:* In the schools we studied, we found no clear and substantial evidence of students increasing their academic achievement as a result of using information technologies.

- *Unexpected outcome:* The overwhelming majority of teachers employed the technology to sustain existing patterns of teaching, rather than to innovate.
- *Unexpected outcome:* Only a tiny percentage of high school and university teachers used the new technologies to accelerate student-centered and project-based teaching practices. (Most preschool and kindergarten teachers already used such practices.)

I am not arguing that teachers seldom change what they do in their classrooms. Teachers continually change their classroom practices. For example, some teachers quickly adopted computers for their classes, though most did not. Yet the teachers who decided to wait or chose to ignore the new technologies still engaged in changing other aspects of their teaching. Some may have decided to use a new textbook; others may have discovered a new way to do small-group work; and even others may have borrowed a technique from a colleague down the hall to press students to write more than a paragraph. These small changes are incremental and occur frequently among teachers. But these small adjustments are not what the promoters of computers had in mind. They wanted to transform teaching from the familiar teacher-centered approach to one that required the teacher to play a considerably different role. Using technology, the teacher would organize the classroom differently, giving students far more control over their learning (for example, working in teams on projects). Such changes would entail fundamental shifts in the teacher's and students' roles, the social organization of the classroom, and power relationships between teacher and students.

The point, then, is that teachers change all the time. It is the kind of change that needs to be specified. Champions of technology wanted *fundamental* change in classroom practice. The teachers that we interviewed and observed, however, engaged mostly in incremental changes. Only a tiny band of teachers moved toward deeper, major reform.[7] These findings and outcomes will disappoint champions of better and faster technology in schools, especially those in Silicon Valley who have heavily promoted major investments in reforming schools through high technology.

THREE QUESTIONS

In the past when innovations aimed at changing classrooms have yielded disappointing results, reformers have often turned first to lapses in teachers' knowledge and skills in explaining why the outcomes were unsatisfactory. Hence, I begin my explanation of these unexpected outcomes by asking three questions about teachers' responses to technological innovations.

1. Are these Silicon Valley teachers' responses to computers similar to or different from other teachers' responses to earlier technological innovations? If these Silicon Valley teachers are similar to those from earlier generations of teachers across the country who faced technological innovations, then explanations for the unintended consequences would need to go beyond these particular teachers' beliefs about technology to account for the similar patterns. If, however, teachers' responses in the past to new technologies differ from these Silicon Valley teachers, then I would need to concentrate on Valley teachers' individual characteristics, school conditions, and other features of the Valley itself to account for the differences.

2. Are these Silicon Valley teachers' responses to computers similar to or different from the responses of other profession-als facing technological innovations? If teachers are similar to other professionals confronting new technologies, then, again, explanations for use and nonuse would have to go beyond Valley teachers' responses to computers and examine other factors. If, however, teachers reacted differently to new technologies, then a close examination of teaching as work would have to be undertaken.

3. *In light of the answers to the previous questions, how do I explain these unanticipated consequences of new technologies in schools and classrooms at the turn of the twenty-first century?* Faced with such evidence of apparent waste in resources, concerned citizens, policymakers, researchers, and practitioners naturally want to know why teachers aren't using the machines for instruction and why students aren't learning more, faster, and better.

As framed, these questions place the problem at the feet of teachers. Answers to these questions become explanations for teachers' classroom behavior when they are faced with technological innovations. Those explanations quickly get converted into solutions aimed at changing teachers' actions in their classrooms. So what I call explanations are really solutions-in-waiting to problems framed by those who invest in new technologies.

To sum up: these unexpected consequences arising from access and use of new technologies in schools attract policymakers' attention because the monies invested in technologies have yet to produce the desired outcomes. Policymakers partial to new technologies in schools view the unanticipated outcomes as problems. Problems need solutions. An explanation of why the problem occurs often contains the seeds of a solution. And this is why explanations are important to policymakers, practitioners, researchers, and informed citizens. Answers to these three questions frame the remainder of this chapter.

QUESTION 1

Are these teachers' responses to computers similar to or different from the ways that teachers responded to earlier technological innovations? In a previous study, I investigated teachers' responses to the introduction of the technological innovations of film (1910s–1940s), radio (1920s–1940s), and instructional television (1950s–1980s). Each of these highly touted electronic marvels went through a cycle of high expectations for reforming schools, rich promotional rhetoric, and new policies that encouraged broad availability of the machines, yet resulted in limited classroom use.[8]

The cycle of attempted change invariably began with extravagant claims for the revolutionary power of films or instructional television to transform teaching and learning. Reformers, including public officials, vendors, foundation executives, and school administrators, fastened onto the new technology, promoting it as a solution for school problems. For example, in the 1950s promoters of instructional television hailed that new technology as a solution to a teacher shortage at that time.[9]

As school boards and superintendents adopted policies and allocated dollars to secure new technology, few teachers were involved either in policy deliberations or in designing how new machines were to be distributed and used. Even without direct involvement, small bands of pioneering teachers begged for funds to acquire the school's first film projector, radio, or television monitor. These champions of technology influenced peers. Not too long after the projectors, radios, and monitors appeared in schools, academic studies established that teachers using new technologies were just as effective, as measured by students' achievement test scores, as teachers using conventional practices.

But logistics gave teachers a headache. Securing a film from the district's audio-visual center at just the right time for a particular lesson or having the radio or television broadcast available at only one time and not other times caused problems. Incompatibility between the existing curriculum and the offerings of films, radio, and television further reduced use. These growing complaints from teachers about inaccessibility and incompatibility stained the mantle of acceptance that had begun to settle over the innovation.

Soon surveys documented teachers' infrequent and limited of film, radio, and instructional television in the classroom. Based on these surveys, I estimated that since 1920 fewer than 5 percent of teachers used these technologies at least once a week. A larger number, perhaps 25 percent, were occasional users (at least once a month); the rest were nonusers. More precisely, teachers' and students' exposure to these technologies outside of school (which were already pervasive in this period) did not influence their use in classrooms.[10]

In classrooms where the new equipment was used, some teachers found that particular films or television programs motivated students to read the textbook, complete worksheets during the school day, and do assignments. Other teachers used the audio-visual equipment to give themselves a tiny break from the tough grind of constant interactions with students over a six-hour school day. In most cases, teachers used the new technology to maintain existing practices.[11]

Both administrators and teachers were criticized for failing to take advantage of powerful technologies that would, promoters claimed, greatly enhance both teaching and learning. Thus the cycle of high expectations, acquisition of new machines, and actual use of the technologies ended with disappointment and recriminations among reformers.

Much evidence over the last decade documents a similar cycle in the Silicon Valley schools' responses to information technologies. As before, public officials and school administrators rarely involved teachers in either the decisions to purchase and deploy computers or the designs for the technology's use in the school. Computers just suddenly appeared on teachers' desks and in special rooms set aside to house the machines, and then reformers watched in dismay as the machines sat idle.

One difference from earlier cycles of change, however, is that teacher are seldom directly blamed for this unexpected outcome. Instead, in the 1990s, public officials, corporate executives, vendors, and administrators call for better college preparation of teachers, improved technical support, and increased professional development to help teachers integrate software into daily instruction. Though the language is nonaccusatory, these calls for helping teachers are still, in Donald Norman's words, a "blame and train" strategy. By asking teachers to redouble their efforts, we take the spotlight off poorly designed hardware and software and inhospitable organizational structures that constrain teacher use.[12]

The answer, then, to the question of how earlier generations of teachers responded to film, radio, and instructional television is that they reacted much like Silicon Valley teachers did when faced with computers. A few "innovators" persuaded "early adopters" to champion the new technology among their colleagues, followed by a very slow penetration into the majority of the teaching corps. Finally, even "laggards" joined the majority of teachers in using films and television; but uses in classrooms were infrequent, limited to maintaining customary practices, and peripheral to the daily routines of teaching and learning (save for a tiny fraction of teachers).[13]

From this glance backward at earlier generations of teachers, I can understand that their limited use of film, radio, and television equipment and programming had much to do with limited access. But Silicon Valley teachers in the 1990s have far more training and far greater access to information technologies, both at home and at work, than earlier generations of teachers were afforded. Today, the state of California requires new teachers to be computer literate, and the culture of Silicon Valley promotes and rewards technological changes that are intended to make teaching and learning faster and better. In such a place, I would expect a more intense use of computers in classrooms. The unexpected similarity in responses of past and present generations of teachers to the new technologies of their day presents a puzzle that I will return to later in the chapter.

QUESTION 2

Looking not backward, now, but sideways, I next ask: *Are these teachers' responses to computers similar to or different from those of other professions facing technological innovations?* Engineers, military leaders, corporate managers, physicians, journalists, publishers, architects, and other professionals have followed the classic S curve in adopting new technologies: the enthusiasm of a few innovators is followed by early adopters, leading to gradual acceptance among mainstream professionals, and then a slow embrace by the last holdouts.[14]

Because there are few studies of how engineers, military officers, physicians, lawyers and other professionals conduct their daily work lives, it is hard to determine similarities or differences between teachers' responses to information technologies and that of other professions. Moreover, it is difficult to generalize about an occupation. Engineers, for example, vary among themselves—mechanical, aeronautical, electrical, civil, and software engineers have different needs and adopt technologies in different ways. Added to that are major differences in institutional goals and structures: a small start-up software company's response to technology is in many ways irrelevant to that of a large urban high school. Nonetheless, a brief inquiry into two occupations noted for their marked embrace of technological innovations and whose workplaces, routines, and incentives are vastly different from school teaching may offer clues to teachers' responses to new technologies. The occupations are engineers and physicians.

Engineers

The little that social scientists know about how engineers go about their work comes from a few researchers who have studied product design, development, and manufacturing. A few case studies (including ethnographies) reveal much about daily routines in varied settings but seldom describe the technologies that engineers use or the actual work they do, except for a handful that examine particular technologies.[15]

What emerges from these studies of different kinds of engineering specialties is that the adoption of new technologies—whether it is a fully integrated robotized assembly cell that puts together interior panels for commercial aircraft or a photovoltaic cell that improves a solar energy system—is a social, political, and organizational process.[16] The social and organizational differences among engineers refer to the status differences between those in design (high), development (middle), and production (low) and the gap in status between professionals and production workers. Moreover, administrators and supervisors possess more authority than engineers—they often interrupt engineers in their work—and often choose what new technologies or software should be purchased and used by the engineers.

A manager at a large firm pointed out the traditional demarcations among engineering and construction in a southern California industrial company with departments using Computer-Aided Design (CAD). "Construction says 'engineering doesn't know what the hell they're doing,' and Engineering would say, 'Construction are those overweight, stogie-smoking, get-down-to-the-brass-facts, don't-follow-the-plans-if-I-don't-have-to kind of people.' And engineers always felt—not always—but the typical attitude might be, 'it doesn't matter what I put on these drawings because Construction's going to build it the way they wanna build it anyway.'[17]

One senior design engineer working in a midsize company building industrial turbine engines described a portion of his work. "When you're doing the mechanical design work, you have to be very aware of all the people that are interfacing and need to work with your design problems. You've got to leave room for the electrical people to put their stuff. You have to know how to put a package together so it can be built in the cheapest, most inexpensive way that you can possibly do. And to do that you are in contact a good portion of the time with other departments."[18]

Political negotiations continually color relations between managers and engineers in and among divisions and departments in a large firm. For some multilevel companies whose past successes have caused them to grow much larger and whose ability to respond quickly to market changes is reduced, entrepreneurial managers have developed a "skunkworks" strategy of innovation. The term comes from Lockheed Aircraft Corporation, which in the 1950s put together an elite group of the best talents in aviation, provided them with a mission and complete creative freedom, and equipped them with every tool they needed to accomplish the job. In short order, the Skunk Works, as this crack team was called, developed the U-2 jet aircraft, and it has continued to be a world leader in avionics innovation for over half a century. (The Skunk Works got its name from the "Skonk Works" of Al Capp's *L'il Abner* comic strip, where a moonshine still was hidden in a secluded hollow.)[19]

Tracy Kidder, in *The Soul of the New Machines,* described how the first 32-bit minicomputer at Data General was designed and built in the late 1970s using a skunk-works strategy. He portrayed engineers working on the secret project within the company as cheerleaders for technology who worked long hours in isolation while their project leader scrounged around for the resources they needed and buffered them from political battles within the company.[20]

Being able to fathom what top corporate executives want and what will pay off for engineers and managers become essential survival skills. In one large successful aircraft company, the divisional operations manager said: "Large or small expenditures in the division . . . had to meet the three informal rules that managers knew by heart guided corporate decision making: 'curb costs, increase productivity, and lose heads (i.e., reduce assembly workers)."[21]

Within these large, midsize, and small companies, engineers used old and new technologies. Old technologies used by design engineers such as pen and paper to draw sketches and bench-built prototypes were as common as new technologies such as CAD-CAM (Computer-Aided Design and Computer-Aided Manufacturing) software. One researcher studied a large company whose top managers had purchased CAD-CAM. The new software builds a picture of a machine and provides the detailed pieces for design and manufacturing engineers to create, develop, and produce turbine engines. To help the conceptual design engineers learn the software, managers arranged two weeks of classes on a half-day basis: 4 hours of regular work and 4 hours of instruction each day. Training time was insufficient; experienced CAD operators outside the company had taken up to 6 months to learn the system's intricacies as applied to their products. Moreover, when designers did play with the system to learn it better, bugs in the software led to lost time and deep frustration with the new technology.

For experienced engineers, hand drawing remained more efficient, and they dropped the CAM part and used the CAD portion of the software in ways unanticipated by the vendor and company managers. As one engineer reported, "We design things on paper, and then hand it over to the CAD system. We use the CAD system as a record keeping, and rather expensive, fast eraser . . . We go backwards. Instead of building a picture and then taking the detail pieces off, we often end up going the other way around—which is wrong."[22] Company engineers facing a new technology that executives had chosen often ended up reinventing the tool to fit the existing organizational structures; as they did so, the relations among engineers and between departments also changed. Mutual adaptations occurred. From design to production, engineers engage in a process that is social, political, and organizational. It is also fragmented, seldom linear, and filled with uncertainty. Such a process frustrates and goads engineers to adapt new and old technologies again and again in order to complete projects.

The conditions under which engineers work differ dramatically from those of schoolteachers in space, control over available time, supervision, and evaluation. Moreover engineers, unlike most teachers, use advanced and complex technologies constantly. Yet what emerges from these few studies of engineers are strong similarities to teachers. If design engineering in a company, for example, is a social, political, and organizational process, so is teaching. In schools, teachers in their self-contained classrooms are organized by grades or departments. They negotiate daily with students, colleagues, administrators, and occasionally parents. Like design engineering, which depends heavily on relationships between engineers and their managers and among engineers themselves in different parts of a company, teaching requires satisfactory relationships between students and teachers, among teachers themselves, and between teachers and administrators. If uncertainty is a hallmark of the journey in engineering from a drawing to a prototype to an actual product being shipped to customers, teaching surely has its daily surprises and unpredictable occurrences.

Finally, and perhaps most important for this analysis, like teachers, engineers selectively adopt, reinvent, and ignore new technologies to fit the workplace and the character of the work itself.

Primary Care Physicians

From what realms of knowledge do most primary care physicians and family practitioners draw to help their patients? Most draw on their clinical experience and knowledge of diseases to determine the value of diagnostic tests or the effectiveness of various treatments and to make predictions about patient's future health. The assumption is that prior training and common sense married to clinical experience are sufficient to allow a clinician to evaluate new diagnostic tests, treatments, and guidelines for practice. If physicians are stuck even after reflecting on their experience and biological knowledge of disease, they often turn to textbooks, recent journal articles, or local experts.[23]

Critics of medical practitioners point out that clinicians lean too heavily upon their idiosyncratic experiences and fail to consult in a systematic way the database of research studies available. First, without the benefit of a control group, it is impossible to tell whether a particular therapy was responsible for a patient's improvement or if the natural history of the disease would have brought about the same result without any intervention. Second, clinicians form impressions about what happened to former patients that permit them to estimate success but that hardly reflect actual rates of abated illnesses. Third, doctors, like most other professionals, want to believe that their diagnoses, therapies, and interactions help rather than harm patients. Thus unsystematic and anecdotal clinical knowledge is given higher priority than research-produced knowledge.[24]

Beginning in the early 1980s, Evidence-Based Medicine (EBM) was designed to help practitioners tap the constantly expanding database of scientific studies and treat patients in a more systematic manner. As one of the innovation's advocates said: "Evidence-based medicine builds upon, rather than disparages or neglects, the evidence gained from good clinical skills and sound clinical experience." When doctors engage in systematic searches of the literature and incorporate findings into their daily work with patients, such work "keeps . . . clinicians up to date and effective."[25]

The innovation calls for family or general practitioners to access (via computer) the massive electronic database of research studies (MEDLINE, American College of Physicians Journal Club on CD-ROM, Cochrane Database of Systematic Reviews on CD-ROM, and so on) when treating patients with earaches, ingrown toenails, hypertension, and mysterious lumps in their abdomens. Once relevant studies have been electronically retrieved, especially those that include randomized clinical trials, the practitioner must critically appraise the studies to determine applicability to the particular patient. As the movement to persuade primary care physicians of EBM's value has spread, guidelines to help practitioners assess the worth of studies have been developed and disseminated through an increasing number of publications, professional development programs for practitioners, hospital resident programs, and medical schools.[26]

David Slawson recounted a story about his patient, a 43-year-old woman who had been admitted to an emergency room suffering from pneumonia. The emergency room doctor wanted to hospitalize her just to be safe. It occurred to Slawson to ask about the benefits to the patient of staying in a hospital. He told the doctor he would get right back to him. A family practitioner at the University of Virginia, he went to his desktop computer and entered data on the woman. With a few clicks of the mouse he found the "prognosis calculator." Slawson determined that her odds of dying in the hospital would be 2.2 times higher (from exposure to germs and possible medical errors) than her odds of dying at home (from complications of the disease). He called the emergency room doctor and gave him the information that he had found. The doctor wrote a prescription and sent her home—saving her insurer, Slawson points out, thousands of dollars and, perhaps, hastening her recovery.[27]

What is missing from this best-case example is the pressured pace of daily encounters between family practitioners and their patients, and the continuing uncertainties that still mark the practice of medicine, either in solo or group practice or as part of a health maintenance organization (HMO). Primary care physicians who see 100 or more patients a week make upwards of 20,000–25,000 clinical decisions a year. As one British family practitioner put it: "I am already struggling with budget managers, contracts with secondary care [providers], and prescribing costs. I hardly have enough time to see all of my patients, let alone do the educational stuff I am supposed to do. And now you want me to look up a reference in some electronic library thing whenever someone comes in with an earache?" Another physician made the same point: "Busy clinicians are now caught in an information paradox: overwhelmed with information but unable to find the knowledge they need when they need it."[28]

The few studies of family practitioners and other physicians using computers for access to relevant studies bear out the time pressure and the tensions facing doctors in finding the best treatment for their patient, reducing costs, and juggling the many other tasks expected of general practitioners. David

Sackett, using studies of self-reported time that hospital-based physicians in the United States and Great Britain have to review journals, concluded that they have about 30 minutes a week for reading. Sackett believes that EBM can still occur, even within that small window of available time. He and his colleagues found that among British general practitioners, a range of 31 to 53 percent of the treatments they used fell into his definition of EBM. This is much higher than among U.S. non-hospital-based practitioners where, again, only a few studies have been done.

For example, Covell and his colleagues concluded in a study of doctors' practices that of all the questions which arise when physicians examine patients, they pursued only about 30 percent of them. Curley and colleagues also found that the criteria practitioners used to determine whether they took the time to investigate other sources to answer questions arising from their patients were practical: which source of information was least costly to acquire, most accessible, and easiest to use?[29]

One study of U.S. rural and urban nonacademic practitioners (unusual in that it depended upon observations, interviews, and follow-up phone calls rather than self-reports) found that clinicians pursued 56 percent of the questions they judged most likely to have answers, compared with 13 percent of those least likely to have answers. These doctors used medical textbooks and clinical manuals (49.5 percent), consultants and colleagues (40.5 percent), and computer searches (2 percent).[30]

Although such limited use of computers to find information might have disappointed advocates of EBM, a 1998 study would give champions of the innovation even more discomfort. A survey was sent to almost 500 family practice residency programs in the United States to determine if they have electronic medical record systems. Most of the systems include information about patient demography, their files, assessments, and plans for care. Many also include an array of database searches that could be used for EBM. Because the Institute of Medicine of the National Academy of Sciences had recommended adoption of electronic records systems by the year 2000 and because residency programs are usually hospital and university based (with access to the latest information technology), one would reasonably expect such systems to be fairly widespread.[31]

The researchers found that 80 percent of the residency programs had never used an electronic medical record system. Only 17 percent of the programs currently use such a system, and 3 percent reported using a system but discontinuing it because of cost and unreliable software. Writing as advocates, the investigators still acknowledged that, in their own residency program, family practitioners argued that "dictating a chart note or writing prescriptions by hand is simpler, less time consuming, and as complete as the electronically captured document." After analyzing the results, the authors concluded that computerized systems are "beset by the dilemmas of up-front and on-going costs, technological realities . . . [and] user resistance."[32]

Admittedly, these studies are few. Nevertheless, what little evidence there is confirms that busy clinicians try hard to help their patients while both facing demands for cost-effective treatments and coping with the uncertainties of the progress and regress of disease. Nevertheless, these studies reveal practitioners choosing to adapt EBM, use it minimally, or ignore it.[33]

Summary of Answers to Two Questions

There is credible evidence, limited to be sure, that teachers' use of computers in Silicon Valley, an area marked by strong support for innovation and technological progress, is similar to earlier generations of teachers facing new machines that also promised much improvement in teaching and learning. With less evidence but enough to make a plausible claim, I have also shown that engineers and physicians noted for their embrace of technological change (and who labor in workplaces quite different from that of teachers) have, like teachers, been very selective in their daily uses of technology, picking and choosing among those new ones that they can adapt most easily to traditional practices. Silicon Valley teachers' use of new technologies, then, duplicates the history of the occupation's response to earlier machines and shares patterns of use with practitioners in very different professions.[34]

These answers to my questions weaken the blame-filled explanations given for teachers' limited and infrequent classroom use of technologies that promised to transform instruction. Explanations anchored in stereotypes of teachers as being more interested in interpersonal relations than in machines, or being by nature technophobic or reflexively opposed to change, fail to account for the vast majority of teachers who have become serious users of computers at home—outside the workplace. Nor do such explanations capture the enthusiasm for learning more about technology that teachers regularly express on surveys and interviews. Finally, these explanations ignore teachers who have become serious technology users at school, to the point of modifying common teaching practices.

QUESTION 3

In light of the answers to the previous questions, how do I explain the unanticipated consequences of new technologies in schools and classrooms that have emerged so clearly in the early years of the twenty-first century? Explaining collective and individual teacher behaviors in using or not using technological innovations needs to go beyond popular explanations that tend to blame teachers for who they are and what they do. Alternative explanations consider personal choices and professional satisfactions interacting with the organizational, political, and social contexts in which people work.

Although the explanations that I offer below differ considerably from one another, they are not mutually exclusive. They overlap while retaining their distinct ways of accounting for the puzzling consequences arising from this study. I begin with the "slow revolution" explanation.

The Slow Revolution

This explanation says that small changes accumulating steadily will create a gradual transformation in how teachers teach. The 1980s and 1990s were only the initial stages of a long revolution that will eventually press teachers to increase the frequency, breadth, and integration of advanced information technologies into their classroom routines.[35]

James Beniger takes the long view in *The Control Revolution.* He points out that there have been four "control revolutions"—that is, humans inventing new technologies to achieve control over their environment. The agricultural revolution almost 10,000 years ago, the commercial revolution a millennium ago, and the industrial revolution 200 years ago are three instances. The commercial revolution followed technical innovations in navigational equipment that permitted Europeans to explore Asia, Africa, and the New World. Governments subsidized colonization and commercial ventures and grew wealthy from the riches that flowed from their colonies. The control of information shifted from handshakes to commercial paper, from personal connections to large bureaucratic companies and government—all to achieve larger economic and social purposes. The "computer revolution," according to Beniger, is only the most recent of a series of technological and economic changes by which information is collected, stored, processed, and communicated to achieve control.[36] The economist Paul David takes a similar but foreshortened view in concentrating upon the past two centuries. He points out that during the Industrial Revolution in the United States, all of the technical developments for commercial applications of electricity occurred by the 1880s, but it was not until the 1920s that companies used dynamos to harness electric power to manufacturing, production, and distribution of products. There is, he argues, an inevitable lag between an invention and its commercial application.[37]

Information technologies are in only the first half-century of their evolution and, like the dynamo, will trigger slow-motion changes in our institutions. Consider that the invention of airplanes in the early twentieth century rendered trains obsolete, but not immediately. Passenger railroads did not begin to decline until after World War II. More than a half-century passed before travelers came to prefer air travel over train travel.[38]

The slow-revolution explanation is easily applied to schools. Technological changes take far longer to implement in formal education than in businesses because schools are citizen-controlled and nonprofit. As systems, they are multipurpose, many-layered, labor-intensive, relationship-dependent, and profoundly conservative. Their primary mission is to make the next generation literate, prepare it for civic duties, and imbue it with the core values of the community. Determining when and whether schools are successful in achieving these purposes is often contested; it depends on what graduates make of their lives and how much of that can be attributed to schools, how much to family upbringing, and how much to other factors that affect both teaching and learning.

Even with these differences between schools and businesses and the lag time between invention and widespread application, over the decades teachers have indeed changed their classroom practices. In the 1930s, for example, increasing numbers of elementary school teachers began using small-group instruction to teach reading. In the 1960s many teachers experimented with different ways of teaching math. Teachers have also slowly adopted technological innovations such as overhead projectors and videocassette recorders (VCRs). And as we have seen, in the 1980s and 1990s pioneering technology-users such as preschool teacher Esperanza Rodrigues, high school humanities teacher Alison Piro, and Professor of English Lawrence Friedlander have integrated information technologies into almost every aspect of their curriculum.

Over the years, then, many teachers have come to embrace some version of an innovation even to the point of teaching very differently from the ways they did before. The incremental process of adopting innovations to the point of reaching a critical mass of teachers, however, had often taken decades rather than a few months or years. Moreover, classroom implementation varied greatly from school to school and from teacher to teacher, because teacher beliefs, community expectations, and structures of age-graded schools, then and now, have been slow to change.[39]

Under a slow-revolution explanation, teachers' adoption of personal computers for classroom preparation and communication, along with the evolution of "hard" and "soft" infrastructures, are early signs of deep changes to come. The evidence of limited use that I have offered, proponents of this explanation claim, merely reflects limited classroom access to new technologies. Once teachers have 4–6 machines and an array of software in their classrooms, a profound shift in teaching practices will occur. Changes will accumulate in upcoming decades much like other innovations—small-group teaching, reading and math innovations—in which teachers altered their core classroom practices. Within another half-century these changes in teachers' beliefs, practices, and infrastructure will spread to most teachers. By then, technologies will have been thoroughly integrated into the daily classroom routine and, as promoters seek, teaching will have shifted from the prevailing teacher-centered to a student-centered practice.[40]

The slow-revolution explanation is plausible. Its incremental view is clearly anchored in the belief that technological change in the larger society inexorably reshapes all institutions, including conservative ones such as schools. Today's toddlers and children, who are quick with games and home computers, will press their parents and teachers unrelentingly toward greater home and school use of electronic teaching materials. If readers sense a technological determinism embedded in the explanation, they would be correct.

Still, this explanation has shortcomings. Why did the availability of new technologies in the 1990s lead most teachers to use computers at home far more than for instruction at school? Why, when teachers did become users, did most continue their customary teaching practices rather than adopt new ones? Nor does this explanation help us make sense of the sudden explosion in wiring, purchase of equipment, provision of technical support, and infusion of professional development in the 1990s. Turning to an explanation that concentrates on contextual factors may help account for these shortcomings.

The Historical, Social, Organizational, and Political Contexts of Teaching

A second explanation for the unintended consequences emphasizes the societal role that schools perform in a democracy, the structures and work roles educators perform, and both the symbolic and actual nature of the technological innovation. These external contexts dynamically interact with internal ones to influence teaching practice. This explanation locates the gap between home and school uses of technology in the social and political organization of schooling, societal expectations for schools, and historical legacies, all of which influence what occurs in classrooms. Furthermore, this explanation tells us why teacher users of information technologies have continued rather than changed routine instructional practices. If the slow-revolution explanation emphasizes change over time, this explanation stresses the overall stability in teaching practices.

I begin with the striking emergence of a large, diverse ad hoc coalition seeking to replicate in public schools the technological transformation that had occurred in the corporate workplace. In the background, but of primary importance, was the state of the economy. The recession of 1991–1992, with an unemployment rate of almost 8 percent and an astonishingly high budget deficit, damaged the incumbency of George Bush and helped elect Bill Clinton as President. The easing of the recession ushered in the longest peacetime economic expansion of the twentieth century. By 2001, almost eight years of high employment, low inflation, and increased productivity—in part spurred by the explosion of technological innovations and further automation of the workplace—had turned the huge federal deficit piled up in the 1980s and early 1990s into federal and state surpluses. By the mid-1990s a growing economy was pumping money into public schools, an institution utterly dependent upon taxes from varied sources.[41]

But why schools? Beginning in the mid-1970s, critics, especially those from the private sector, connected America's loss of global markets to Japan and Germany with the poor academic performance of American students and the unbusinesslike approach that educators took in schooling America's children. The argument that economists and corporate leaders used again and again was that the United States would find it hard to outstrip Japan or other countries in productivity unless its schools produced literate and skilled graduates for the workforce. And that, they said, was exactly what schools were failing to do.[42]

Soon federal and state policymakers joined the chorus of criticism by setting national goals for public schools, raising academic standards, mandating tests to determine that the standards were being met, and holding principals, teachers, and students accountable by rewarding high test scores and punishing low ones, just as any efficiently run business would do. Dependent on sustaining the political legitimacy that public schools have had in the past, educators could do little more than protest details of the criticism and climb on board the popular movement to improve schools' productivity. By the end of the twentieth century, standards-driven policies that called for states to test every student repeatedly, publish the scores, and hold teachers and administrators responsible for student's academic performance had swept the nation. One tool to achieve that higher productivity, according to corporate and public officials, was the introduction of new technologies into the classroom.[43]

The American public has largely endorsed this business model for school improvement. By most measures, parents have expressed steady and increasingly strong support for computers both as learning tools in their own right and as critical preparation for a future workplace. In one 1995 public opinion poll, 75 percent of respondents agreed that "computers have improved the quality of education." In another poll of voters two years later, 92 percent said that a school that is "well-equipped with computers" has a "very major advantage" over a poorly equipped school. In that same poll, voters believed that well-equipped schools had the advantage over less-endowed schools in "preparing students to enter the workforce" (92 percent), "making learning a more active experience" (86 percent), and "providing more individualizing attention" (70 percent).[44]

Public officials and corporate leaders experiencing an expanding economy increasingly driven by technological changes used the popular critique of schooling to justify large investments aimed at making schools high-tech institutions. Although it would be preferable to attribute expenditures for technologies to rational deliberations among public officials and corporate leaders, the broad support for new technologies in schools across all sectors of society suggests that more was involved than rational decision making. The reasons given for wiring schools and investing in equipment reveal less concern over whether the computer was effective in raising achievement or transforming learning and teaching than over the perceived imperative of simply getting machines into schools. Decisions to purchase hardware and software or wire schools were as much symbolic political gestures as they were attempts to actually acquire the right tool to get a job done well.[45]

By the late 1990s, the computer—like past mechanical marvels such as the steam engine, the railroad locomotive, and the airplane—had become, among other things, a high-status symbol of power and modernity. Within mainstream American culture in the decades preceding the twenty-first century, being "modern" meant being efficient, productive, businesslike, innovative, and forward-looking. Even the term "high tech"—like high fashion, high church, high class, high society—conveys an aura of superiority relative to other "low tech" methods and materials.[46]

For public school officials who rely on the good will and political support of voters, failure to redirect budgets toward building a technological infrastructure for teachers and students could be political suicide. Even with little evidence that investments in information technologies raise test scores or promote better teaching, most school managers use the rhetoric of technological progress to establish legitimacy with their patrons and the private sector. Similarly, university presidents, like public school boards and superintendents, are dependent on elites and various stakeholders for political and financial support. These institutions' very legitimacy depends, in part, on demonstrating to donors, legislatures, alumni, parents, and voters that the universities are fulfilling their dual mission of creating and disseminating knowledge. Woe to the school leader unable to show patrons and visitors rooms full of machines. A "good" school has become, by definition, a technologically equipped one.[47]

HISTORICAL LEGACIES IN SCHOOL
STRUCTURES, ROLES, AND ACTIVITIES

The university, like the American kindergarten and the comprehensive high school, is about a century old, although its antecedents can be traced to the early decades of the nineteenth century.[48] By the turn of the twentieth century, many antebellum colleges had dissolved their religious ties and embraced a secular mission committed to both teaching and research.[49] In continuing to admit undergraduates, however, these emerging universities had to contend with the religiously based moral mission of the antebellum college that charged professors to build student character and cultivate citizenship—the teaching imperative. Facing this dilemma of reconciling research with teaching, presidents of these turn-of-the-century universities invented a compromise: the university-college.[50]

Within this organizational structure, the mission of teaching and minding the moral life of undergraduates became embedded within discipline-based departments, the elective system, and required liberal arts courses called "general education." Yet it soon became clear to new and veteran professors alike that any classroom innovations which expected changes in teaching practice would subtract valuable time from doing research. Thus, in accommodating new technologies into their daily work, it is unsurprising that most university faculties used computers much more for their research agendas rather than for teaching courses.

When school districts established high schools in the mid-nineteenth century, they chose as their model the small liberal arts college. District school boards approved curricula that prepared students for college, encouraged high school teachers to copy professors' pedagogies, and endorsed organization into departments even to the point of recruiting teachers trained in separate academic disciplines. As the purposes of high school expanded to prepare students for industrial and commercial job markets, to build citizens, and to mold character, vocational departments, extracurricular activities, and student government were added. By the 1920s, the comprehensive high school as we know it today had emerged.[51] We can see these trends clearly in the case of Las Montañas High School. The local district school board and superintendent establish how large classes will be in each of the schools and allocate the appropriate funds. The superintendent monitors high school principals, who in turn oversee department heads working with individual teachers. The 1,300 students and 60 teachers at Las Montañas are divided into departments and have a daily schedule of six periods, each 55-minutes long.[52] The structure of the six-period school day makes it difficult for teachers trained in separate disciplines to engage in school reforms, including integrating new technologies that ask them to cross subject-matter boundaries and team-teach with other faculty members. On two occasions, the Las Montañas faculty deliberated about changing the daily schedule to make it more flexible, and twice the teachers rejected a proposal to end the six-period day.

Other structures and external demands, often unseen and taken for granted, affect the way technology is used, or not used, in classrooms at Las Montañas. State and district requirements for graduation, age-graded organization, departmental boundaries, secondary teachers' disciplinary training, and self-contained classrooms all combine to reduce cross-fertilization of ideas within and across departments and to encourage teachers to behave as academic specialists whose primary concern is covering the body of information contained within a textbook in 36 weeks. That most district and high school administrators decided to centralize school computers into labs and media centers rather than equip individual classrooms reflects, in part, available monies and, in part, the preferences of already harried academic teachers. Feeling that new technologies were an add-on to an already over-extended workday, those teachers wanted the autonomy to decide whether to take their classes to the media center or computer lab or stay put in their lower-tech classrooms. Yet despite the powerful legacies of the past in unforgiving contexts, a small but hardy band of Las Montañas teachers did nevertheless become serious computer users and made deep changes in how they taught.

History and context also matter for preschools and kindergartens. With the slow spread of private preschools throughout the twentieth century, an ideology and practice of early childhood education became embedded in the social organization of these schools.[53] With its rug for circle time, toys, sometimes a small kitchen area, a wash basin, bathroom, cubbies for coats and cuddlies, and discrete learning centers located in various parts of the room, no one could mistake a kindergarten for a high school or university classroom. Parents came to expect a homelike setting with a caring teacher who was closer to a mom or dad than to a subject-matter specialist. They also expected the teachers to inculcate the virtues common to family and community life: being honest, respecting authority, helping others, sharing what you have, and cleaning up your own mess.

Educators' strong beliefs in how best to develop a young child's intellectual, social, physical, and emotional sides led to smaller classes in preschools and kindergartens than those in upper grades, playlike activities that cultivated each child's talents, and a teacher knowledgeable about children's stages of development and interests. The social organization of the classroom reflected these evolving beliefs. Each classroom had a teacher who expected each child to grow at his or her own pace through individual and group work and play, through activity centers and group tasks, while acquiring the skills and knowledge necessary for later school success. The teacher's role was to integrate various activities into a seamless web of lessons while walking the fine line between classroom order and individual freedom. The job also meant taking time to listen to each child's story, wipe away every tear, and share each small victory. If individual student choice and exploration, rather than mandatory activities and homework, ruled these settings, children still knew that the grown-ups were in charge.

Within this overall homelike atmosphere, computers have made few ripples. Adding a computer station to the existing learning centers—the water table, blocks, dress-up closet, climbing structure, book corner—expanded what children could choose to do and gave tangible evidence to both teachers and parents that the school had begun to help young children on the road to computer literacy. But no standard computer curriculum has evolved: the software that gets loaded on computers in a given school depends a great deal on what is available and on the school's academic or nonacademic orientation.

Contexts, past and contemporary, external and internal, shaped, in part, what occurred in early childhood programs, comprehensive high schools, and the university with respect to using computers for instruction. But there is another contextual factor that teachers themselves pointed out to us repeatedly: flaws in the technology itself. Since the nineteenth century, chalk and blackboard, pens, pencils, and textbooks have proven themselves over and over again to be reliable and useful classroom technologies. Teachers added other innovations such as the overhead projector, the ditto machine (later the copying machine), and film projector (later the VCR) because they too proved reliable and useful. But most teachers continue to see the computer as an add-on rather than as a technology integral to their classroom content and instruction.

Policymakers and practitioners commonly see these old and new technologies as value-neutral devices, that is, as tools that can be used for good or ill. The evidence in schools, however, increasingly makes clear that wiring schools, purchasing computers, networking machines, and using the machines themselves are hardly value-free behaviors. Social practices accompany every technology, from electricity to the telephone, automobile, and airplane. Certain rules and procedures must be followed that slowly change the organizational, political, and cultural context of a classroom, not to mention a school.[54] It is, in part, because of the potential of these new technologies to alter existing social practices of teaching and learning that teachers at all levels have expressed ambivalence about these powerful machines. Repeatedly, for example, administrators, coordinators, teachers, and students otherwise committed to using computers mentioned inadequate wiring, servers crashing, constant upgrading of obsolete software and machines, and insufficient technical support. Serious teacher users who were ardent pioneers of technology said that on any given day they had to have a back-up lesson plan, just in case the Internet search, on-line curriculum, Power-Point presentation, or word processing program disappeared because a server went down or was running too slowly. The unreliability and complexity of the technology undermined teacher confidence in its practical benefits. Even at schools with technology coordinators and rapid-response student assistants on-site, not all the troubles teachers experienced could be fixed immediately. On many occasions, teacher requests for help overwhelmed on-site support personnel.[55]

But a deeper analysis goes beyond the annoying breakdowns and basic unreliability. A few of the teachers and coordinators we talked with pointed to vendors who sell machines and software each year that are bigger, faster, and flashier but have little to do with what teachers want for their students. Donald Norman, former Hewlett-Packard executive and Vice President of Apple Computer, calls such company practices "rampant featurism." He is unsparing in his criticism of the personal computer's defects.[56]

"Do you think," Norman says, that "311 commands is a lot for a word processing program?" Microsoft Word had that many commands in 1992. Five years later, the same program had 1,033 commands. Was the program easier to use, he asks? "Of course not." Like the teachers, Norman knows that computer companies make their money by creating software that gets increasingly complex, requiring faster machines with more memory. When schools (and other organizations) can't keep up with the costs of software, hardware, and wiring capacity, more crashes and glitches develop. The lesson Norman draws from rampant featurism is the importance of simplicity in design and use. The lesson I draw is that computers carry enough baggage with them to reshape the practice of schooling; they are hardly neutral tools.[57]

As consumers of technologies, teachers have no say about rampant featurism. Moreover, corporate marketing practices invariably produce incompatibilities between wiring, software requirements, and machine demands. Seldom have teachers been asked what works best for them in various circumstances with different students. Because technology vendors sell to administrators, teachers often end up using machines that are far too complex for their classroom needs. For example, many of the software applications used in schools (such as spreadsheets and databases) were created for professionals in business. These applications required design features different from those teachers would need for teaching and learning. There is, as Ronald Abate says, a tool mismatch. The interaction between the new technologies, vendor claims, and the goals teachers strive to reach and the structures within which they work has created deep ambivalence among teachers, administrators, and students about what these machines and software can and cannot do.[58]

As with the slow-revolution explanation, the history-and-contexts explanation is plausible. The past really does exist in the diverse goals of public schooling, present school structures, organizational roles, and decision-making processes. All of these affect what teachers in their classrooms do at various levels.[59] What is missing, however, from each of these explanations is a straightforward answer to these two questions:

- Why did a small number of teachers become technological innovators?
- And why, among those early adopters, were there other teachers who then used computers to move from largely textbook-bound, teacher-centered practices to more intellectually demanding, complex forms of practice?

Because the prior explanations fail to account for these mavericks, I offer a final one.

CONTEXTUALLY CONSTRAINED CHOICE

As constrained as teachers are by the history and contexts in which they work, they still exert substantial discretionary authority in their classrooms. In age-graded schools with self-contained classrooms, teachers become gatekeepers for what content and skills are taught and how they are presented to their students, whether the students are 4 years old, 14, or 24. Although few teachers control class size and determine which students present themselves on the first day of school—district, state, and university administrators make those decisions—yet teachers do decide how the space, furniture, and time are to be used in their classroom. They decide how to group students and to what degree and under what circumstances students participate in class. They decide what instructional tools (texts, machines, and so on) best meet their goals for learning and what content in which order should be taught.

These are weighty decisions to make, and teachers' beliefs and attitudes about how students learn, what they should know, what forms of teaching are best, and the purposes of schooling all get factored into teacher decision making. Despite the constraints of context, teachers act independently within their classrooms.[60]

In the case of information technologies, teachers make choices by asking practical questions that computer programmers, corporate executives, or educational policymakers seldom ask. And the reason is straightforward enough: schools serve many and conflicting purposes in a democratic society. Teachers at all levels have to manage groups in a classroom while creating individual personal relationships; they have to cover academic content while cultivating depth of understanding in each student; they have to socialize students to abide by certain community values, while nurturing creative and independent thought. These complex classroom tasks, unlike anything software developers, policymakers and administrators have to face, require careful expenditure of a teacher's time and energy. So in trying to reconcile conflicting goals within an age-graded high school or a bottom-heavy, research-driven university, teachers ask themselves down-to-earth questions in order to decide which electronic tools they will take to hand. Here are some of the questions teachers ask:

- Is the machine or software program simple enough for me to learn quickly?
- Is it versatile, that is, can it be used in more than one situation?
- Will the program motivate my students?
- Does the program contain skills that are connected to what I am expected to teach?
- Are the machine and software reliable?
- If the system breaks down, is there someone else who will fix it?
- Will the amount of time I have to invest in learning to use the system yield a comparable return in student learning?
- Will student use of computers weaken my classroom authority?[61]

Drawn from the everyday experiences of teachers in preschools through graduate schools, these practical questions have a gritty merit to them that few vendors or educational policymakers distant from classrooms and unmindful of the varied social purposes that tax-supported schools serve could ask. Nevertheless, I suspect that other professionals, including engineers and physicians, ask similar practical questions of new technologies every day.[62]

The situational autonomy that both novice and experienced

teachers have in classrooms means that choices are made daily. The beliefs and values that teachers hold drive many of the choices they make in the classroom. The satisfaction they gain from student learning and the interpersonal relations that grow daily are high on most teachers' lists. In a 1996 national poll, for example, 76 percent of teachers said that it is essential for students to display "curiosity and a love of learning." When that curiosity and learning occur, teachers glow.[63]

Teachers, and those who write about teaching, often talk about the "joys of teaching," "the teachable moment," and the occasional prickly sensation on the back of one's neck when an antagonistic student accepts the help of a teacher or when a group of students volunteer to work after school on a project. Between teachers and students, emotional and intellectual exchanges occur. Trust and affection evolve into life-long, cross-generational friendships. These relationships are deeply satisfying to teachers. They are, in Dan Lortie's words, the psychic rewards of teaching.[64]

Earning those psychic rewards depends a great deal on the contexts that teachers interact with and the range of beliefs and attitudes they have about teaching and learning. These contexts, beliefs, and attitudes vary considerably. Some teachers want to teach in just the way their favorite elementary or high school teacher did. Others are motivated by a desire to be just the opposite of their worst teacher. Many teachers believe in high academic standards, demanding homework, whole-group discussion, and lecturing. Many teachers believe that the way to engage students is with small-group work, structured choices, individual projects, and hands-on activities. And many teachers construct hybrids of these differing beliefs.[65]

Although a teacher's mindset may not steer all of his or her classroom actions—because of organizational and other contextual factors—they clearly influence how the classroom is organized for instruction and how teaching is approached. Beliefs influence where teachers decide to teach, what and how they choose to teach, the satisfaction they achieve in their classrooms, and the degree of dissonance, even conflict, they feel and express when their values are compromised.

The maverick computer-using teachers I have identified—Alison Piro, Esperanza Rodrigues, Mark Hunter, and Lawrence Friedlander—sought to substantially change their instructional practices. They welcomed computers with open arms, took courses on their own, incessantly asked questions of experts, and acquired the earliest computers available at their school or for home use. They did so because they sensed that these machines fit their pedagogical beliefs about student learning and would add to the psychic rewards of teaching. Most of the innovators used computers to support existing ways of teaching. Others not only embraced the new technology but also saw the machines as tools for advancing their student-centered agenda in transforming their classrooms into places where students could actively learn.

Thus, even within the constrained contexts in which teachers found themselves, teachers—as gatekeepers to their classrooms—acted on their beliefs in choosing what innovations to endorse, reject, and modify.

SUMMING UP

The introduction of computers into classrooms in Silicon Valley schools had a number of unexpected consequences. They are:

- Abundant availability of a "hard" infrastructure (wiring, machines, software) and a growing "soft" infrastructure (technical support, professional development) in schools in the late 1990s has not led, as expected, to frequent or extensive teacher use of technologies for tradition-altering classroom instruction.
- Students and teachers use computers and other technologies more at home than at school.
- When a small percentage of computer-using teachers do become serious or occasional users, they—contrary to expectations—largely maintain existing classroom practices rather than alter customary practices.

Explanations that indirectly or directly blame teachers collectively for infrequent use of new technologies and sustaining existing practices even when there were machines available are inadequate. In examining how earlier generations of teachers responded to new electronic technologies and exploring how engineers and family practitioners adapted to new technologies, I concluded that there were similar patterns in responses to new technologies from teachers then and now and from practitioners in very different professions.

The three explanations I offered (slow revolution, history-and-context, and contextually constrained choice) easily meet the test of plausibility. But a plausible explanation is neither necessarily credible nor persuasive. Because explanations contain the seeds of policies (that is, each explanation offers a solution to a policy problem), it is important to close the gap between plausibility and credibility.

The slow-revolution explanation is appealing, especially for those who believe in the inevitability of technological progress. Simply put, more and more teachers will become serious users of computers in their classrooms as the "hard" and "soft" infrastructures mature in schools. This explanation also suggests that uses of technology to preserve existing practices will continue among most teachers but give way slowly to larger numbers, especially as high schools and universities shift to more student-oriented teaching practices.

For the tiny band of teacher-users who have already transformed their classrooms into student-centered, active learning places, the slow-revolution explanation places them in the vanguard of a movement that will eventually convert all classrooms into technology-rich sites. Embedded in the explanation is a supreme confidence that with further work to secure better equipment, more training, and adequate technical support, as the years pass a critical mass of users will accrue, and the gravitational force of this group will draw most of the remaining teachers into technology's orbit.

Although the slow revolution can be persuasive in taking the long view to explain some of the unintended consequences we found in our study, this explanation is silent about the surge of spending on technology in schools in the 1990s and not a decade earlier or later. Nor does this explanation account fully for both teachers' and students' broader (and more frequent) use of technologies at home and office than at school. Both young and old seemed to have learned quickly to use the new technologies at home. Why not at school? It is a question not easily turned aside by the comment that this discrepancy, too, will disappear in time.

The history-and-contexts explanation suggests more complex, deeply embedded factors that will continue to retard widespread classroom use of technology. For example, the web of traditional social beliefs held by taxpayers, parents, and public officials about teaching and learning, and the broader historic purposes schools serve in a democracy have a powerful influence on what educators think and do. Also consider how economic prosperity and recession expand and reduce the revenues flowing into the public schools, ultimately influencing what is available for spending on new technologies and technical support, reducing class size, building more preschools, broadening professional development, and designing innovative programs.

In the high schools we observed, two outcomes become understandable through the history-and-contexts explanation: teachers' higher use of computers at home than in classrooms, and (among those who use computers for instruction) a tendency to adapt technology to support existing teaching practices rather than alter them.[66] Consider the historical constraints imposed on high school teachers—even the most techno-enthusiastic among them: the separate classrooms, individual departments, age-graded groupings, and six-period work day. Add the time spent by each teacher to work out the logistics necessary to bring classes to media centers and computer labs. Then factor in nervousness over possible server crashes, software foul-ups, printer glitches, and slow Internet connections. Any high school teacher who manages to use computers in the classroom has somehow overcome a host of organizational obstacles, political decisions made by others remote from the classroom, and difficulties associated with the technology itself, including mismatches between "rampant featurism" and the teacher's practical needs in the classroom.

In preschools and kindergarten, the historical residue of early childhood ideology, classroom organization, and teacher practices nicely accommodated one or two classroom computers within the familiar schedule that has children going to various activity centers for part of the day. Although some teachers may have had reservations about young children using computers, for the most part those reservations dissolved in the limited contact that 4- and 5-year-olds had with computers. Most early childhood teachers already were committed to active learning, direct experience, and projects. They already structured their classroom space and activities to encompass the children's intellectual, social, and emotional development. In effect, they maintained their existing student-centered practices while using computers.

Within the university, the invention of the university-college, bottom-heavy decentralization, and structural incentives and rewards drove most professors to value research more than teaching. These facts of university life constrained most professors from investing the time required to use computers for teaching but not from embracing them for use in their research, in preparing for lectures, and in communicating with colleagues and students. Except for a small group of professors, then, most would continue to teach as they had before the introduction of computers. Moreover, the administrators and technologists who designed strategies to introduce new machines involved few, if any, professors in their decisions to purchase and deploy computers.

The interplay between historical, organizational, economic, social, political, and technological contexts has much explanatory power. What occurred in these varied settings was a mutual adaptation between workplace demands on teachers, what they found useful in the technologies, and the institutional arrangements.[67] Yet both the slow-revolution and the history-and-context explanations fail to account for the small cadre of teachers who went against the mainstream to become serious users of computers at home and school. Nor do these explanations account for a few mavericks who embraced the new technologies to create classrooms where students inquired more deeply into subjects, crossed disciplinary boundaries, and experienced learning in ways they had seldom encountered in schools. It is the explanation of teachers making contextually constrained choices that highlights why small bands of teachers acting autonomously used computers to transform their classrooms.

Although I am tempted to combine the different explanations into one that covers all of the unanticipated outcomes I have identified, I resist that lure. Yes, the slow revolution is compelling simply because any parent, researcher, or policymaker who has gone into schools repeatedly over the last decade can see the obvious increase in computers. Yet the ardent promoters' chain of logic that access will lead to widespread use and use will transform teaching and learning has yet to be realized in Silicon Valley schools. I find compelling the combined explanations of historical legacies and the contextually constrained choice of teachers in accounting for the patterns of teacher and student use in different levels of schooling. The two explanations, taken together, persuade me. Even if every single child had a personal computer at home and in school in the next decade or half-century as a consequence of the slow revolution, I believe that core teaching and learning practices—shaped by internal and external contexts—would remain very familiar to those who would visit mid-twenty-first-century schools.

In the final chapter I elaborate my position by examining advocates' claims for reforming schools through technology and the implicit policies buried in the three explanations and answer the question: Are computers in schools worth the investment?

6

ARE COMPUTERS IN SCHOOLS WORTH THE INVESTMENT?

"Think of a company where the CEO has control of less than 2 percent of the budget. Where he can't hire or fire his staff, and where it's very hard to measure outcome. Would you invest in a company like that?" For John Doerr, a Silicon Valley entrepreneur whose firm has invested in scores of technology start-ups, the company above is a public school and its CEO is the principal. His answer was an emphatic no.

By the late 1990s, Doerr and other venture capitalists had welded together an amply funded political coalition that lobbied state and federal officials to reform public schools through technology, higher academic standards, and accountability. In this final chapter, I pursue the larger implications of what I found in Silicon Valley, offering answers to the question that John Doerr asked and the one that I pose as the chapter title.[1]

OUTCOMES

What should be clear to impartial observers of new technologies in American schools is that after twenty years of heavy promotion, serious investment of funds, and unswerving support from a disparate coalition of parents, corporate executives, public officials, and educators, computers are ubiquitous in schools. In urban, suburban, and rural classrooms, media centers, and labs, they are as familiar an icon of schooling as homework and classroom clocks. Although some disparities in Internet connections still exist between schools with low-income students and affluent suburban enrollments, these inequities in access are slowly dissolving. Champions of computers in schools, each group seeking different goals, can take pride in a stunningly swift victory in broadening student access to these powerful technologies in schools across the nation.[2]

Success in making new technologies available obscures, however, the divergent goals spurring the loosely tied coalition. Some promoters sought more productivity through better teaching and learning. Others wanted to transform teaching and learning from traditional textbook lessons to more learner-friendly, student-centered approaches. And some wanted students to become sufficiently computer literate to compete in a workplace that demanded high-level technological skills. Have these varied purposes been achieved in schools?

Beginning with computer or digital literacy, more and more students now take required keyboarding classes and courses in computers that concentrate on learning commonly used software. No consensus, however, exists on exactly what computer literacy is. Among computer advocates, definitions diverge considerably. Is it knowledge of and skill in programming? Is it being able to trouble-shoot computer lapses or software glitches? Is computer literacy knowing how to run popular software applications such as word processing programs and spreadsheets? Or is it simply completing a required course in computers? When we remember the many shifts in the meaning of computer literacy since the 1980s (recall how experts once urged everyone to learn BASIC programming), any hope of securing agreement on a common definition appears slim. On such an elementary but crucial point, promoters offer little direction to computer-using teachers.[3]

Some researchers have claimed that computer literacy, however defined, pays off in higher wages, further strengthening the educational rationale for using computers in schools. Yet schools can hardly claim full credit for students' growing technological literacy, when many also pick up computer knowledge and skills at home and in part-time jobs. The contribution that school courses and experiences have made to computer literacy and competitiveness in the workplace remains, at best, murky.[4]

As for enhanced efficiency in learning and teaching, there have been no advances (measured by higher academic achievement of urban, suburban, or rural students) over the last decade that can be confidently attributed to broader access to computers. No surprise here, as the debate over whether new technologies have increased overall American economic productivity also has had no clear answers. The link between test score improvements and computer availability and use is even more contested.[5]

Nor has a technological revolution in teaching and learning occurred in the vast majority of American classrooms. Teachers have been infrequent and limited users of the new technologies for classroom instruction. If anything, in the midst of the swift spread of computers and the Internet to all facets of American life, "e-learning" in public schools has turned out to be word processing and Internet searches. As important supplements as these have become to many teachers' repertoires, they are far from the project-based teaching and learning that some techno-promoters have sought. Teachers at all levels of schooling have used the new technology basically to continue what they have always done: communicate with parents and administrators, prepare syllabi and lectures, record grades, assign research papers. These unintended effects must be disappointing to those who advocate more computers in schools.[6]

Securing broad access and equipping students with minimal computer knowledge and skills may be counted as successes. Whether such intended effects lead to high-wage jobs is unclear because the outcomes may be due more to graduates' skills picked up outside of school or to their paper credentials. When it comes to higher teacher and student productivity and a transformation in teaching and learning, however, there is little ambiguity. Both must be tagged as failures. Computers have been oversold and underused, at least for now.

Suppose, however, that policymakers took the explanations for why widespread access to new technologies in schools seldom led to frequent use in classrooms and converted the explanations into policy prescriptions. Might far-reaching reform in teaching and learning then occur?[7]

According to the slow-revolution explanation, it is premature to call the investment in computers in schools a failure because of a lack of evidence for increased productivity and transformed teaching and learning. As the infrastructure matures and teachers' beliefs about teaching and learning evolve, more and more teachers will change their practices and become serious users of computers in their university and public school classrooms. For policymakers and practitioners who find such an explanation convincing, certain policy directions follow:

- Speed up the process of making computers readily available to students in each classroom.

- Eliminate the gap in Internet access between urban and suburban schools.
- Invest more in online curriculum and distance learning.
- Increase on-demand technical support for teachers.
- Add more professional development.

In short, accelerate the change by helping teachers do now what they will be doing anyway in a few years. Since the mid-1990s, the public policy endorsed by most corporate promoters, civic officials, and educators has embraced this approach.[8]

Yet the history-and-contexts explanation challenges the slow revolution assumption that increasing availability will eventually lead to increased use of computers in public school and university classrooms. According to this explanation, school structures and historical legacies carry so much weight that, unless changed, they will retard widespread use of technology and hinder substantial changes in classroom practices. Implied within this explanation is an ecological approach to change, where technologies, individuals, networks of social relationships, structures, and political actors interact and adapt to one another, further strengthening the durability of existing practices.[9]

For policymakers and practitioners considering this explanation, the implications demand far more comprehensive and systemic actions than merely adding more resources and teacher training. Solutions would have to address the ecology of schooling:

- Plans would have to be made now for fundamental changes in how elementary and secondary schools are organized, time is allocated, and teachers are prepared.
- Hardware manufacturers, software firms, and telecommunication

companies would need to develop software and equipment specifically designed for teachers and students.

- They would have to improve product reliability to limit the defects in their wares, increase technical support to teachers, and test software on consumers before marketing it to district and state administrators.

- The special needs of urban schools and the low-income communities in which these schools are often located would require sustained attention to the links between the economic, social, housing, and political structures of the neighborhood and the quality of schooling.

Without such major changes in the basic structures and processes that have influenced both urban and suburban teaching practices for many decades, only minor alterations in classroom practice will occur, no matter how much money is sunk into information technology.

In the mid-1980s, just at the time techno-enthusiasts turned their attention to schools, there were determined efforts to restructure both urban and rural public schools to prepare a foundation for more ambitious forms of instruction and curriculum. Initiatives in elementary and secondary schools across the country sought to realign the age-graded school, bridge subject-matter boundaries, share decision making in schools, and increase teacher collaboration to achieve professional communities where learning was intellectually rigorous, active, and project-based. Within a few years, however, the surge of restructuring ebbed, and a new generation of school reformers promoting rigorous academic standards, accountability, and higher test scores gained prominence. Few national and state reformers have yet to champion the restructuring of age-graded schools and similar ventures.[10]

In universities, beginning in the late 1980s, coalitions of faculty, students, and administrators sought to improve the quality of undergraduate education and, specifically, to realign the historically subordinate role of teaching relative to research. Senior professors started teaching seminars with first- and second-year students, teachers received cash awards for excellent teaching, administrators evaluated teachers according to new criteria, centers for the improvement of teaching cropped up, and "research" was redefined to incorporate teaching. Teaching through technology, online curriculum, and distance education topped the reformers' list of efficient ways to reshape undergraduate education and give teaching more salience. Because few of these novel efforts altered the university-college system or the prevailing incentives embedded in academic rank, tenure, and promotion, the influence of the innovations on university teaching has been marginal.[11]

For preschools and kindergartens, contexts also mattered, but the implications drawn for universities and secondary schools hardly apply to these early childhood settings. No major alterations in the structures, processes, and belief systems of teachers are necessary to accommodate computers. The organizational, social, and political contexts reinforced by the history of these classrooms for both affluent and poor 3- to 5-year-olds already support more complex forms of student-centered instruction. The social organization of the classroom and dominant norms of teaching, learning, and appropriate child development readily provide a comfortable niche for new technologies. Because teachers are (and have been) the gate-keepers to what enters their preschool and kindergarten rooms, such shared beliefs and a common approach to early childhood development has meant that few disruptions occurred in adding one or two computers to the existing array of learning centers.[12]

While the history-and-contexts explanation can partially account for the underuse of computers in the classroom, it does not give adequate weight to the discretion of individual teachers as gatekeepers to their classroom. Even though teachers and, to a limited degree, professors are constrained by their lower position in the hierarchy of school authority and by the web of social relationships among students, other teachers, parents, and district officials, they nonetheless make choices. They are, for example, still consumers of technology. They ask practical questions about the details, logistics, and worth of new technologies in their classrooms. Their questions must be openly asked and answered. Implied in the contextually-constrained-choice explanation, then, is the following policy recommendations:

- Policymakers and administrators must understand teachers' expertise and perspectives on classroom work and engage teachers fully in the deliberations, design, deployment, and implementation of technology plans.[13]
- The structural constraints that limit teacher choices in high schools and universities must be reduced, and a more relaxed schedule with large chunks of uninterrupted time for joint planning, crossing of departmental boundaries, and sustained attention to different forms of learning must be implemented.
- The infrastructure of technical support and professional development would need to be redesigned and made responsive to the organizational incentives and workplace constraints teachers face.

Although there is much talk of respecting teacher expertise, recognizing exemplary teachers, and appointing occasional teachers to blue-ribbon commissions, most teachers historically have had little say in designing and implementing technology plans. Even fewer teachers design professional development programs specifically targeted toward their peers. When teachers do engage in such deliberations and when they design programs for themselves, when their opinions are seriously considered, changes in classroom practice occur that even the teachers themselves had not contemplated.[14]

There are, fortunately, a few instances of reformers taking teachers' perspectives seriously, especially in using technologies that build programs around their classroom expertise. One federally funded project explicitly built a five-year teacher-led technology program aimed specifically at creating more student-centered classroom practices than previously existed in the district. There may well be other similarly inclined programs, but this one I came to know well.[15]

THE TEACHER-LED TECHNOLOGY CHALLENGE PROJECT (TLTC)

By 2000, TLTC had completed the full cycle of equipment delivery, installation of machines, teacher staff development, and technical support for all Berkeley Unified School District (BUSD) elementary and middle schools. The project goals, design, and implementation were straightforward. Director Harvey Pressman wanted teachers to use computers in their classrooms daily. He sought to have teachers integrate the technology into their curricular and instructional routines. The logo of the project said it all: "It is not about technology; it is about learning."

The kind of learning that Pressman and his staff wanted was

largely student-centered practices that would help all students, particularly those who were largely poor, minority, and with special needs. He called these students "struggling learners" and saw that they could profit from the harnessing of technology to everyday lessons. District officials deeply concerned about low test scores welcomed all of the equipment, professional development, and concentration on the school site and on struggling learners.

The superintendent and school board swiftly approved the project. Without access to new equipment or any ongoing district-wide program of professional development (each school decided with their local funds what in-service programs they would pursue), the Teacher-Led Technology Challenge Project was manna from heaven.

TLTC's strategy was to place two multimedia computers, a scanner, and a printer in the 175 classrooms in 15 schools. Other equipment for the school included a digital camera and software programs for all grades. Each school was assigned an Instructional Technician (IT) on site to help all teachers with hardware and software problems. In each school, a teacher volunteered to be a Lead Teacher for one year. Lead Teachers, without a reduction in their classroom responsibilities, helped the other teachers integrate software and computer activities into daily lessons. The project provided staff development to prepare the Lead Teacher and other faculty. Finally, there was a TechnoKids component in which students could take home a computer to have their families use the machines.

In each of the initial years, four to five schools were invited to participate in the project. At each school, one third of the faculty was formally trained during the year with TLTC providing school-based workshops using substitute teachers to release those who attend the sessions, one-on-one help in the teacher's classroom, and other resources to build the capacity of each teacher to use the hardware and software as part of the daily curriculum. At the end of three years, each school's entire faculty had received training in using computers in their classrooms. After the third year, TLTC funding for the Lead Teacher, technology, and on-site professional development ended.

The project is completing its final year and seeking ways to institutionalize its main features (computers in each classroom, integration of software use into daily lessons, teacher-led professional development, and on-site instructional technicians) into the Berkeley Unified School District's regular programs. District officials have realized that TLTC has become a de facto system-wide professional development program not only for using technology in classrooms but also for expanding student-centered teaching practices. They also note that a cadre of experienced Berkeley teachers have become committed to integrating computers into daily classroom activities to create student-centered classrooms. These teachers lead workshops for other Berkeley teachers. In short, a critical mass of Berkeley teachers have been school site and district leaders in advancing learning through technology.

At the end of the project's third year, an external evaluation had documented that 20 to 40 percent of the teachers credit TLTC with "increasing their use of student-centered practices such as cooperative learning and differentiation of instruction for students of different learning styles and abilities." Teachers reported to evaluators that the majority of their students benefited from participation in TLTC in increased technical skills, added interest in school, and more cooperation with other students. The district has yet to make achievement test scores available to the evaluators, so no correlation between computer use and test score data is known. The TechnoKids program had a slow start, and by the end of the third year computers had reached only 300 students' homes out of almost 4,400 in TLTC classrooms.[16]

It will take far more than five years for most Berkeley preschool, elementary, and middle school teachers to be comfortable integrating technology into daily lessons. The reasons stem less from a slow-revolution explanation than from a history-and-contexts one. Because it was federally funded and temporary, TLTC could do little to alter the entrenched social, organizational, and political contexts of the Berkeley schools. For example, the decentralization of professional development and fiercely protected autonomy of each school were deeply held political values converted into structures that were seldom questioned, yet they undeniably shaped school-by-school responses to TLTC.

As TLTC withdraws its resources, the question of how many of its key features will be retained arises. Each Berkeley school has district funds available for its use. Each staff has to decide whether on-site information technology is worth the cost and whether the school should invest in more professional development for computer-using teachers determined to make learning and technology a seamless web. Past experience with federally funded innovations that slipped off into limbo when funding ended leads one to predict this as a likely scenario for Berkeley and TLTC.

In an unlikely but desirable scenario (from the view of the director of TLTC), selective adaptation of TLTC features would be funded by individual schools or schools that pool their resources. And in another even less probable scenario, district leadership would mobilize support for institutionalizing the teacher-led, school-site driven features of TLTC. Which scenario or combination of scenarios will unfold for this uncommon project remains uncertain. Without serious attention directed toward the commonplace contexts in the Berkeley schools, however, it is unlikely that the TLTC strategy will outlast the life cycle of new computers.

CRITICALLY EXAMINING REFORMERS' ASSUMPTIONS ABOUT TECHNOLOGY

Unlike Pressman and TLTC, most advocates for computers have seldom taken seriously teachers' classroom experiences, expertise, or the constrained choices that teachers face. Promoters of new technologies inside and outside schools who have moved past the popular explanations for teachers' limited and infrequent use of computers (such as resistance and technophobia) might find the slow-revolution and history-and-contexts explanations plausible, even credible. But these reformers intent upon increasing teacher use of computers in schools might better profit from analyzing their own implicit beliefs about technology.

For example, most reformers seem to assume that earlier investments in technologies have been worth the cost and that further investments are necessary for expanding and integrating teacher and student use of technologies into schooling. Entangled in this core premise are two corollary assumptions. The first is that wiring schools and creating the hardware and software infrastructures that give students and teachers access to technology will solve most of education's problems. Yet the most serious problems afflicting urban and rural poor schools—inequitable funding, extraordinary health and social needs growing out of poverty, crumbling facilities, unqualified teachers—have little to do with a lack of technology. The second corollary is that access to more and faster information means that students will become knowledgeable. The thrill of retrieving hard-to-get information quickly is a long stretch from thoughtfully considering the information and turning it into knowledge or, in time, forging that knowledge into wisdom. Critical awareness, reasoning, and judgment are basic skills that transform information into knowledge. No cheaply and swiftly acquired information can substitute for these critical faculties.[17]

The billions of dollars already spent on wiring, hardware, and software have established the material conditions for frequent and imaginative uses of technology to occur. Many students and teachers have acquired skills and have engaged in serious use of these technologies. Nonetheless, overall, the quantities of money and time have yet to yield even modest returns or to approach what has been promised in academic achievement, creative classroom integration of technologies, and transformations in teaching and learning. Nor can proponents of a slow revolution be confident that those outcomes will materialize without considerable changes in school organization, respect for teacher expertise, and the distribution of decision-making authority among teachers, administrators, and policymakers.

It is seldom noted publicly, but many promoters of new technologies seem to have forgotten the historic civic idealism and broad social purposes public schools serve in a democracy. Well-intentioned reformers eager to make schools efficient instruments of American global economic competitiveness speak mostly about standards-based curriculum, test scores, and accountability as portals through which students move to become workers and consumers who help expand markets and contribute to soaring profits. They concentrate upon how schools serve the economy and how much individuals can gain, rather than on the public good. Recapturing the broad democratic purposes that Americans have sought through schooling and the critical importance of the schools in building and sustaining social capital challenges the assumptions passionately held by promoters of technology in schools.

SOCIAL CAPITAL AND TECHNOLOGY

Social capital refers to the connections between individuals that evolve into trust and reciprocity—critical component of any society but especially one that prizes civic duties and democratic virtues.[18] A progressive educator in 1916 first used the phrase "social capital" to press for reform in the state's rural schools. Few reformers or writers then applied it to schools. Today, building social capital is considered essential; as Robert Putnam puts it, "Civic connections help make us healthy, wealthy, and wise."[19]

In his famous article (and now book) entitled "Bowling Alone," Putnam cited evidence that increases in social capital allow citizens to solve collective problems more easily, build trust in both civic and economic transactions, bind them to others whose fates they share regardless of how different they may be, and even contribute to individuals' health and their ability to cope with illness and stress.

Skeptics have questioned the inventory of benefits for the individual, community, and nation that Putnam claims will flow from increased social capital. They point out that the evidence he presents is fragmentary and, at best, only suggestive. What commends his work, however, is its making explicit the crucial connection between building trust and cooperation in a society and keeping democracy vital. Moreover, he is clear on the role that schools play in building social capital. He recommends that students be required to engage in meaningful community service, that school staffs and students build networks with parents and neighborhoods that combine academic learning and participation in community decisions, and administrators deepen extracurricular involvement of students in the community and redesign a civic curriculum.[20]

Regardless of whether Putnam's argument and evidence convince skeptics, the link he makes between school reform and broader civic and social purposes serves to underscore the barrenness of the popular rationale for computers in schools. Driven by economic motives, many technologically inclined reformers seldom have looked beyond linking standards-based curriculum, test scores, and accountability to increasing economic productivity and the Gross National Product. With supreme confidence, they view serious school problems in both cities and suburbs as mere technical glitches, ones they can solve with smarter managers, more machines, cleverer software, adequate staff support, and increased professional development. Quick and cheap access to information will lead, they claim, to more knowledgeable, wiser students. Calls for civic activism and a clear sense of the broader social purposes for schooling that drove earlier generations of reformers are absent from current agendas.

Contemporary reformers have forgotten the democratic mission at the heart of public schooling, ignored the critical importance of social capital in strengthening civic behaviors, and proven too narrowly committed to technocratic solutions of school problems—all of which tempts me to call for a moratorium on buying any more computers for K–12 schools. A moratorium might startle people into openly debating serious questions about how and why computers are used and how they fit in with the larger purposes of universal education. But I know how futile such a gesture would be. Few educational policymakers, practitioners, or parents eager to advance their children's economic prospects can turn their backs on technology, even if they were so inclined. That choice dissolved as computers spread throughout the workplace and the Internet invaded all aspects of mainstream society.[21] To educators dependent on voters and taxpayers for funds and political legitimacy, it often matters little whether the new technology is costly and fully tested to do what vendors and promoters say it can do. Pressed by parents, business leaders, public officials, and computer vendors, few school boards and administrators can resist the tidal wave of opinion in favor of electronic solutions to education's age-old problems. The questions asked are seldom *whether* to move ahead with new technologies but how, under what conditions, and to what degree.

Educators, of course, are not the only ones vulnerable to pressures for more and better technology. In 1983 President Ronald Reagan proposed to use lasers and emerging technologies to create a defensive shield against Soviet nuclear missiles. The proposal led to the Strategic Defense Initiative or "Star Wars" campaign. Even though the technology was then unavailable to shoot down incoming missiles, billions were spent by the Pentagon to develop antimissile technologies. By the early 1990s, no such defensive shield had been erected. Antimissile tests failed time and again. Since the demise of the Soviet regime, billions more were spent by Congress and Presidents Bush and Clinton to develop laser beams and other defensive weapons to foil attacks from nuclear-loaded rockets. A durable coalition of congressional advocates, Pentagon officials, and defense contractors has bridged partisan differences for almost two decades to invest even larger sums in "Star Wars" research and development of antiballistic weapons that have yet to prove successful in tests. What ties together the "Star Wars" initiative and computers in schools is the powerful belief that new technologies can solve any and every problem, even if the machinery has yet to be invented and successfully used.[22]

Given that more and more computers will be bought and a call for a broad-scale moratorium would fail, I would urge that we address the important question: Toward what ends? District administrators committed to technology have to budget large sums to replace aging computers, maintain the existing inventory of machines, provide on-site technical support, and purchase new software. In appropriating substantial funds for sustaining technology in a given district, administrators often leave other pressing needs unmet. A partial list might include:

- smaller class size
- higher entry-level teacher salaries
- renovation of decayed buildings
- responsive school communities
- full-day preschool and kindergarten
- cross-disciplinary programs in the high schools
- innovative arts programs in the elementary schools
- another foreign language for middle school students.

Imagine what a list of such unmet needs would look like for New York City, Los Angeles, Boston, Detroit, or Atlanta. In the zero-sum game that gets played out in most public school districts throughout the nation, expenditures to maintain the infrastructure of technology throughout a district undermine the claim of enthusiasts that technology is not value-free.

Needs, however, are not equivalent to purposes. Public officials and school policymakers are duty-bound to ask tough questions about the civic, social, individualistic, and economic goals that parents and taxpayers expect their schools to reach. Yet few administrators discharge these obligations. Instead, the economic competitiveness and private purposes that different groups of reformers promote have dominated educational debate in the past two decades and distorted the mission of schools and universities. Policymakers, in their unalloyed admiration for the global success of American businesses, have regrettably slipped into a severe amnesia about why schools and universities exist in a democracy.

Yet technology will not go away, and educators have to come to terms with it as an educational tool. Understanding technology and the social practices that accompany it as a potent force in society is incumbent on both students and adults. From the telephone to the automobile to the computer, technologies carry with them the baggage of complex social practices and values that need to be explicitly examined. Therefore educators must ask whether spending our limited educational funds to sustain technology will bring us closer to the larger democratic purposes that are at the heart and soul of public schooling in America? Seldom has this question been openly debated by policymakers, practitioners, and parents. When difficult public choices must be made, policy decisions should be informed by the past, situated in the present, and measured against the overriding civic and social purposes necessary for a democratic society.

How early childhood classrooms, high schools, and universities in Silicon Valley and across the nation responded to the last two decades of technological innovations is a case study in both stability and change. No one who attended schools in the 1950s and then visited schools in 2000 could fail to note many important differences in classroom practice. It is untrue that schools or teachers cannot change. Those visitors, however, would also note strong, abiding similarities between classrooms and teaching practices a half-century apart. Those similarities are due to the historical legacies and contexts. Ad hoc incremental changes have occurred often; fundamental changes have occurred seldom.

Although promoters of new technologies often spout the rhetoric of fundamental change, few have pursued deep and comprehensive changes in the existing system of schooling. The introduction of information technologies into schools over the past two decades has achieved neither the transformation of teaching and learning nor the productivity gains that a reform coalition of corporate executives, public officials, parents, academics, and educators have sought. For such fundamental changes in teaching and learning to occur there would have to have been widespread and deep reform in schools' organizational, political, social, and technological contexts. From my inquiry into Silicon Valley schools I have concluded that computers in classroom have been oversold by promotors and policymakers and underused by teachers and students.

I predict that the slow revolution in technology access, fueled by popular support and continuing as long as there is economic prosperity, will eventually yield exactly what promoters have sought: every student, like every worker, will eventually have a personal computer. But no fundamental change in teaching practices will occur. I can imagine a time, for example, when all students use portable computers the way they use notebooks today. The teacher would post math assignments from the text and appropriate links on her Website, which students would access from home. Such access, however, will only marginally reshape the deeply anchored structures of the self-contained classroom, parental expectations of what teachers should be doing, time schedules, and teachers' disciplinary training that help account for the dominant teaching practices. The teacher in my example would use the laptops to sustain existing practices, including homework. In short, historical legacies in school structures and parents' and taxpayers' social beliefs about what schools should be doing, I believe, will trump the slow revolution in teaching practices. Those fervent advocates who seek to transform teaching and learning into more efficient, productive work through active, student-centered classrooms will find wholesale access to computers ultimately disappointing. Without a critical examination of the assumptions of techno-promoters, a return to the historic civic and social mission of schooling in America, and a rebuilding of social capital in our schools, our passion for school-based technology, driven by dreams of increased economic productivity and the demands of the workplace, will remain an expensive, narrowly conceived innovation. The next generation of Americans will wonder about the wisdom of previous reformers seeking technocratic solutions that ignored the broader civic and social roles of schools in a democratic society.

Should my conclusions and predictions be accurate, both

champions and skeptics will be disappointed. They may conclude, as I have, that the investment of billions of dollars over the last decade has yet to produce worthy outcomes.

For those who make the decisions to buy and deploy computers in schools, it is now time to examine the assumptions propelling reform through technology. It is now time to ask: how do these monies help us achieve our larger social and civic goals? In what ways can teachers use technology to create better communities and build strong citizens? The answers to these questions, as I have argued, are in the minds and hands not only of teachers but of policymakers, public officials, corporate elites, and parents who set the educational agenda. Without attention to the workplace conditions in which teachers labor and without respect for the expertise they bring to the task, there is little hope that new technologies will have more than a minimal impact on teaching and learning. And without a broader vision of the social and civic role that schools perform in a democratic society, our current excessive focus on technology use in schools runs the danger of trivializing our nation's core ideals.

APPENDIX: RATIONALE FOR CHOICES OF SCHOOL LEVELS

Why did I omit elementary and middle schools from this study? For grades 1 through 3, I reasoned as follows. Patterns of technology access and classroom use in the lower grades of elementary school resemble broadly the beliefs and practices observed in most kindergartens. These classrooms exhibit a clear set of beliefs about how young children should learn, how teachers should teach them, and what knowledge and skills are essential in these years. This early childhood ideology is established in preschool and kindergarten and codified by professional associations, teacher education institutions, and administrators.

Although teachers have been under pressure for the past two decades to decrease play and exploration in these classrooms and increase academic preparation for the upper grades of elementary and middle school, they still retain a strong commitment to what professionals call "developmentally appropriate" activities. Hence I claim that examining preschool and kindergarten sites in Silicon Valley for technology access, use, and outcomes does capture in large part what occurs in elementary school primary grades.

For grades 4 through 8, the move to middle schools has created larger buildings than elementary schools where subjects are taught separately, fewer self-contained classrooms hold students for the entire day, students move to different teachers for academic subjects, and the time schedule more closely resembles high school than elementary school. Because most middle schools more closely mirror high school organization and size, I omitted these grades.

But the more important question is whether the evidence of technology access, use, and outcomes for the elementary school years is largely different from or approximately similar to high school. If the evidence shows major differences in access and use between elementary and high schools, then excluding elementary schools from this investigation would be injudicious. If, on the other hand, the evidence displays some differences but shows strong similarities in access and use, then concentrating on high schools would be a reasonable, even if contested, decision.

What does the evidence say? As of 1998, access to computers in elementary schools differed from that in high schools in some respects but overall the two were approximately the same. The ratio of students to computers was just over 7.5 in elementary schools; in high schools it was almost 7. In elementary schools, 56 percent of these computers were in classrooms, 37 percent were in computer labs, and 6 percent were in media centers and other places. In high schools, 42 percent were in classrooms, 49 percent were in labs, and 9 percent were in other places.[1] Internet access varied also. In elementary schools, 24 percent of the computers had high speed Internet access, 26 percent had medium-speed, 37 percent had modem only, and 13 percent had no access. In high schools, 45 percent of the computers had high speed access, 29 percent had medium speed, 24 percent was modem only, and 2 percent had no access.[2]

Although computers were deployed differently in the two settings, elementary schools and high schools were virtually identical in making computers available to teachers and students (93 percent of elementary schools had machines; 91 percent in high schools). Moreover, 22 percent of elementary schools and 31 percent of high schools were technology-intensive schools. Access to new technologies, then, is largely similar between the two levels of schooling.[3]

When it comes to classroom use of new technologies, reports from teachers and students in elementary school do differ from those in high school. For example, in a national survey sponsored by the U.S. Department of Education in 1999, 92 percent of elementary school teachers reported that they used computers at school; 80 percent of secondary school teachers said they did. Among elementary school teachers, 56 percent said their students used the Internet at school, whereas 72 percent of secondary teachers reported the same practice. At home, the percentages of elementary and secondary school teachers using computers were almost the same (83 and 89 percent respectively), as were percentages using the Internet at home (57 percent and 60 percent, respectively).[4]

Elementary and secondary school students taking the National Educational Assessment Program reported in 1998 different frequencies of computer use in their classrooms. Among fourth graders, 29 percent said they used computers once a week in the classroom; among eighth graders, 38 percent; among twelfth graders, 47 percent.[5]

In another national survey of households done by the Bureau of the Census in 1993, nearly 70 percent of preschool and kindergarten children used computers in school, according to a family member. For high school the figure was 58 percent.

In 1997 the percentage of young children using computers in schools, according to a later Census Bureau survey, had climbed to 79 percent, while for high school students it was 70 percent. The census takers also asked about home use and found that, in 1993, 25 percent of elementary-school-aged children used computers at home, whereas 29 percent of high schoolers did so; in 1997, the figures were 43 and 49 percent, respectively.[6]

When outcomes are considered—that is, academic achievement, college attendance, attitudes toward learning, and similar results—neither in elementary nor in high schools do researchers or practitioners offer evidence to show a moderate to strong linkage between student and teacher access and use, or between their use and outcomes.

When I examined classroom studies and ethnographies to see whether these inquiries add or detract from survey results, I made three observations. First, very few researchers enter classrooms to see how teachers and students actually use technology every day. Second, in the few studies that have been done, what teachers said they do with computers in their classrooms varied a great deal from what researchers observed. Teachers tended to overestimate frequency of computer use. This discrepancy between self-report and practice is common not only among teachers but also among other professionals. Third, what occurred in elementary and secondary classrooms with new technologies was largely similar.[7]

On the basis of these mixed reports, I concluded that omitting elementary schools would not substantially alter the findings or conclusions that I drew from preschool and kindergarten and high school classrooms.

NOTES

INTRODUCTION: REFORMING SCHOOLS THROUGH TECHNOLOGY

1. David Tyack and Larry Cuban, *Tinkering toward Utopia* (Cambridge: Harvard University Press, 1995); Michael Fullan, *The New Meaning of Educational Change* (New York: Teachers College Press, 1991); Richard Elmore and Milbrey McLaughlin, *Steady Work* (Santa Monica: Rand, 1988). Larry Cuban, "Reform Again, Again, and Again," *Educational Researcher* 19, no. 1 (1990): 3–13.

2. Henry Perkinson, *The Imperfect Panacea: American Faith in Education, 1865–1965* (New York: Random House, 1968). Carnegie quotation on p. 122.

3. Barbara Beatty, *Preschool Education in America: The Culture of Young Children from the Colonial Era to the Present* (New Haven: Yale University Press, 1995); Nina Vandewalker, *The Kindergarten in American Education* (New York: Macmillan, 1908).

4. National Center for Education Statistics, "America's Kindergartners," February 2000, NCES 2000–070 (Washington, DC: U.S. Department of Education, Office of Educational Research and Improvement, 2000); "Kindergartner Study Finds Four Sectors Far behind the Pack," *New York Times*, February 18, 2000, p. A19.

5. Cuban, "Reform Again, Again, and Again." Epigraph in Perkinson, *The Imperfect Panacea* (n.p.).

6. The National Commission on Excellence in Education, *A Nation at Risk: The Imperative for Educational Reform* (Washington, DC: Government Printing Office, 1983), pp. 5, 7.

7. Thomas Toch, *In the Name of Excellence* (New York: Oxford University Press, 1991); Thomas Timar and David Kirp, "Educational Reform and Institutional Competence," *Harvard Educational Review* 57 (1987): 308–330.

8. For a representative example of these reformers, see David Kearns and James Harvey, *A Legacy of Learning* (Washington, DC: Brookings Institution Press, 2000). Kearns was former chairman of Xerox Corporation (and an Assistant Secretary of Education in President George Bush's administration), and Harvey helped produce the *Nation at Risk* report. They established the privately funded New American Schools Development Corporation in 1991, which promoted different models of school reform.

9. William Reese, "Public Schools and the Elusive Search for the Common Good," and Ted Mitchell, "Turning Points: Reconstruction and the Growth of National Influence in Education," in Larry Cuban and Dorothy Shipps, eds., *Reconstructing the Common Good in Education: Coping with Intractable American Dilemmas* (Stanford: Stanford University Press, 2000), pp. 13–31, 32–50.

10. In a Public Agenda survey, 87 percent of Americans asked said that "a college education has become as important as a high school diploma used to be." Jodi Wilgoren, "Study Finds Most in U.S. See College Education as Essential," *New York Times,* May 4, 2000, p. A21.

11. John Meyer, "Reflections on Education as Transcendence," in Cuban and Shipps, *Reconstructing the Common Good,* pp. 206–222; Cuban and Tyack, *Tinkering toward Utopia.*

12. Neil Postman, *The End of Education: Redefining the Value of School* (New York: Vintage Books, 1996), p. 45; Robert Fulghum, *All I Really Need to Know I Learned in Kindergarten* (New York: IVY Books, 1986), p. 4; David Labaree, "Public Goods, Private Goods: The American Struggle over Educational Goals," *American Educational Research Journal* 34, no. 1 (1997): 39–81.

13. Lawrence Cremin, *American Education: The National Experience, 1783–1876* (New York: Harper and Row, 1980); David Tyack and Elisabeth Hansot, *Managers of Virtue* (New York: Basic Books, 1982).

14. Dorothy Shipps, "Echoes of Corporate Influence: Managing Away Urban School Troubles," in Cuban and Shipps, *Reconstructing the Common Good,* pp. 82–106.

15. David Labaree, *How To Succeed in School without Really Learning: The Credentials Race in American Education* (New Haven: Yale University Press, 1997).

16. Since the mid-1990s, the concentration on high academic standards, raising test scores, and holding teachers and principals accountable for improving student performance on tests has been unrelenting. See David Hoff, "Made to Measure," *Education Week,* June 16, 1999, pp. 21–36.

For Texas and California, two states that have moved aggressively forward in these arenas, see Linda McNeil, *Contradictions of School Reform* (New York: Routledge, 2000), and EdSource, *National Accountability Movement Offers Lessons for California* (Palo Alto: EdSource, Inc., 2000). For a balanced account of the last half-century of tests and their uses, see Robert Linn, "Assessments and Accountability," *Educational Researcher* 29, no. 2 (2000): 4–16.

17. For a typical article describing the different "stakeholders" in a broad coalition endorsing more technology in schools, see Jim Puzzanghera, "High Tech Is Gore's Domain—But He Has Rivals," *San Jose Mercury News*, February 13, 2000, pp. 1, 14A. Corporate leaders supported Net Days held around the country in 1996 and 1997 when volunteers from businesses, government, and education went into schools to network computers, install phone lines, and wire classrooms to the Internet. Larry Slonaker and Howard Bryant, "Rich Get Richer," *San Jose Mercury News*, March 7, 1996, pp. 1A, 21A.

18. Louis Uchitelle, "Productivity Finally Shows the Impact of Computers," *New York Times*, March 12, 2000, p. 4BU. For the long debate over whether computers have increased economic productivity, see W. Wayt Gibbs, "Taking Computers to Task," *Scientific American*, July 1997, pp. 82–89; Jeff Madrick, "Computers: Waiting for the Revolution," *New York Review of Books*, March 26, 1998, pp. 29–33.

19. See Consortium on Productivity in the Schools, *Using What We Have To Get the Schools We Need: A Productivity Focus for American Education* (New York: Consortium on Productivity in the Schools, 1995). Gerstner's speech to the National Governors' Conference (1995), cited in Thomas Glennan and Arthur Melmed, *Fostering the Use of Educational Technology* (Santa Monica: Rand, 1996), p. 9.

20. D. Jamison et al., "The Effectiveness of Alternative Instructional Media," cited in Arthur Melmed, "Productivity and Technology in Education," *Educational Leadership*, February 1983, pp. 4–6. The literature on computer-assisted instruction, integrated learning systems, and tutorial software is filled with studies that demonstrate more student learning through using computers than conventional means of instruction as measured by scores on standardized achievement tests. See Heather Kirkpatrick and Larry Cuban, "Computers Make Kids Smarter—Right?" *Technos* 7, no. 2 (1998): 26–31.

21. Quotation of Steve Case comes from interview in *Business Week*, September 25, 2000. See http://www.businessweek.com:/2000/00_39/b370019.htm. M. Suzanne Donovan, John D. Bransford, and James

Pellegrino, eds., *How People Learn: Bridging Research and Practice* (Washington, DC: National Academy of Sciences, 1999); J. S. Brown, Allan Collins, and P. Duguid, "Situated Cognition and the Culture of Learning," *Educational Researcher* 18, no. 1 (1989): 32–42. Lauren Resnick, *Education and Learning To Think* (Washington, DC: National Academy Press, 1987). For constructivist thinking among university faculty, see "Teaching at an Internet Distance: The Pedagogy of Online Teaching and Learning. The Report of a 1998–1999 University of Illinois Faculty Seminar. 2. The Present Status of Online Instruction," http://www.vpaa.uillinois.edu/tid/report/tid_report.html.

22. As one report put it, "The real promise of technology in education lies in its potential to facilitate fundamental, qualitative changes in the nature of teaching and learning." In the President's Committee of Advisors on Science and Technology, Panel on Educational Technology, "Report to the President on the Use of Technology To Strengthen K–12 Education in the United States" (Washington, DC: President's Committee of Advisors on Science and Technology, March 1997), p. 33. Also see Christopher J. Dede, "Imaging Technology's Role in Restructuring for Learning," in *Restructuring for Learning with Technology* (New York: Center for Technology in Education, Bank Street College of Education, 1990); Barbara Means, *Technology's Role in Education Reform* (Menlo Park: SRI International, 1995); Judith Sandholtz, Cathy Ringstaff, and David Dwyer, *Teaching with Technology* (New York: Teachers College Press, 1997).

23. Susan Hammer, "Our Future," *San Jose Mercury News,* March 7, 1996, p. 9B.

24. Jeff Archer and Mark Walsh, "Summit Garners Mixed Reviews from Pundits, Practitioners," *Education Week,* April 3, 1996, p. 12, 15. Policy statement text is on p. 13 of April 3 issue.

25. U.S. Department of Education, *Getting America's Students Ready for the Twenty-First Century: Meeting the Technology Literacy Challenge* (Washington, DC, June 1996).

26. U.S. Department of Education, "Discounted Telecommunication Services for Schools and Libraries: E-Rate Fact Sheet," June 9, 1998, Washington, DC; Gary Chapman, "Federal Support for Technology in K–12 Education," in D. Ravitch, ed., *Brookings Papers on Education Policy* (Washington, DC: Brookings Institution Press, 2000), pp. 320–321; Anthony Trotter, "Rating the E-Rate," *Education Week,* September 20, 2000, pp. 3–6, 9, 11, 15.

27. U.S. Department of Commerce, Bureau of the Census, *Statistical Abstract of the United States, 1991* (Washington, DC: Government Printing

Office, 1991), p. 150; Market Data Retrieval, unpublished tabulations from 1998–99 School Technology Survey and published tabulations from earlier MDR surveys in "Technology Counts '99," *Education Week,* September 23, 1999, p. 64.

28. In the President's Committee of Advisors on Science and Technology Report to the President (PCAST 1997), pp. 57–66; Kerry White, "A Matter of Policy," in "Technology Counts," *Education Week,* November 10, 1997, pp. 40–42.

29. NPR/Kaiser/Kennedy School Kids & Technology Survey, http://www.npr.org/programs/specials/poll/technology/technology.kids.html.

30. Tracy Seipel, "Firms to Give $100 million for Internet Access," *San Jose Mercury News,* April 18, 2000, pp. 1, 16.

31. See the Appendix for the reasons I omitted elementary schools.

1. THE SETTING

1. Joan Didion, "The Golden Land," *New York Review of Books,* October 21, 1993, p. 86.

2. Peter Schrag, *Paradise Lost: California's Experience, America's Future* (Berkeley: University of California Press, 1998), pp. 281, 282–283.

3. J. S. Holliday, *The World Rushed In: The California Gold Rush Experience* (New York: Simon and Schuster, 1981), pp. 48–49.

4. Quoted in Didion, "The Golden Land," p. 88.

5. John Muir quotation cited in Didion, "The Golden Land," p. 91.

6. Schrag, *Paradise Lost,* pp. 282–283.

7. Bryce quoted in Holliday, *The World Rushed In,* p. 451; Schrag, *Paradise Lost,* pp. 188–198; Kevin Starr, *Inventing the Dream: California through the Progressive Era* (New York: Oxford University Press, 1985), pp. 252–259.

8. Histories of the Santa Clara Valley and how its fruit industries changed into semiconductor and later computer industries can be found in the following works: Michael Malone, *The Big Score: The Billion Dollar Story of Silicon Valley* (New York: Doubleday, 1985); Paul Frieberger and Michael Swaine, *Fire in the Valley: The Making of the Personal Computer* (Berkeley: Osborne/McGraw-Hill, 1984); David Kaplan, *The Silicon Boys* (New York: William Morrow, 1999); also see *San Jose Mercury News* for its 10-part series of events that shaped Silicon Valley. See particularly Willys Peck, "Agriculture's Erosion," December 27, 1999, p. 1A; James Mitchell, "Valley's Corporate Model," December 29, 1999, pp. 1A, 6A; Tom Quinlan, "The Start-Up Culture," December 31, 1999, pp. 1A, 16A.

"Silicon Valley" was first used as a phrase to describe the growing semiconductor industry in the area by Don Hoefler, a journalist, in 1971 (http://www.internetvalley.com/donhoefler-frame-right-0221-1.htm). Langdon Winner, "Silicon Valley Mystery House," in Michael Sorkin, ed., *Variations on a Theme Park: The New American City and the End of Public Space* (New York: Hill and Wang, 1992), pp. 31–33.

9. Winner, "Silicon Valley Mystery House"; figure for rental of billboards comes from Pham-Duy Nguyen, "Signs of Our Changing Times," *San Jose Mercury News,* December 13, 1999, p. E1.

10. Kaplan, *Silicon Boys,* pp. 1–12.

11. "Giving Gap," Editorial, *San Jose Mercury News,* December 19, 1999, p. 6P.

12. Ibid.; Michelle Quinn and Jennifer Lafleur, "Money, Money Everywhere So Why Don't You Feel Rich?" *San Jose Mercury News,* August 15, 1999, pp. 1A, 17–18; Michelle Quinn, "Green, with Envy," *San Jose Mercury News,* August 16, 1999, pp. 1, 8–10A. Kaplan, *Silicon Boys,* p. 15.

13. Quinn and LaFleur, "Money, Money Everywhere," p. 1; Jennifer Mena, "Escaping High Costs: The Goal for Family of Six," *San Jose Mercury News,* August 16, 1999, p. 9A; Yomi S. Wronge, "Boom Bypassing Children," *San Jose Mercury News,* June 2, 2000, pp. 1B, 4B.

14. James Lardner, "World-Class Workaholics," *U.S. News and World Report* 127, no. 24 (1999): 50.

15. Peter Carey and Joshua Kwan, "Prosperity's Shadow," *San Jose Mercury News,* December 26, 1999, p. 20A. Overwork, of course, is common outside of the Valley. See Arlie Hochschild, *The Time Bind* (New York: Metropolitan Books, 1997).

16. Carey and Kwan, "Prosperity's Shadow," p. 20A.

17. D. W. Miller, "Anthropologists Exploring Silicon Valley Find 'The Best, the Brightest, the Greediest,'" *Chronicle of Higher Education,* October 1, 1999, pp. A21–22. Also see Leslie A. Perlow, *Finding Time: How Corporations, Individuals, and Families Can Benefit from New Work Practices* (Ithaca: ILR Press, 1997).

18. Janice Rombeck, "Survey Finds Desire for Neighborhood Ties," *San Jose Mercury News,* December 27, 1999, p. 16A.

19. These beliefs and motives are displayed in vignettes and books on Silicon Valley entrepreneurs, engineers, and venture capitalists. See, for example, Kaplan, *Silicon Boys;* Michael Lewis, *The New New Thing: A Silicon Valley Story* (New York: W. W. Norton, 1999), ch. 8; Freiberger and Swaine, *Fire in the Valley: The Making of the Personal Computer.* In the *Mercury News* poll, 71 percent of those polled agreed with the state-

ment: "The growth of the high-tech industry has created more opportunities than problems." Carey and Kwan, "Prosperity's Shadow," p. 1A.

20. *EdSource Report,* "How California Compares: Indicators and Implications for Our Public Schools," November 1998, p. 1; *EdSource Report,* "School Finance, 1999–2000," November 1999, p. 1.

21. Schrag, *Paradise Lost,* pp. 139–187.

22. Michele Foster, "As California Goes, So Goes the Nation," *Journal of Negro Education* 65, no. 2 (1996), pp. 105–109.

23. Schrag, *Paradise Lost,* pp. 66–87; Michael Kirst and Gary Yee, "An Examination of the Evolution of California State Educational Reform," in Diane Massell and Susan Fuhrman, eds., *Ten Years of State Education Reform, 1983–1993* (New Brunswick, NJ: Consortium for Policy Research in Education, 1994).

24. Kirst and Yee, "Examination."

25. In California, the schools are funded by the governor and legislature, which also establishes policies—the multivolume School Code—for almost 1,000 districts to follow. In addition, the governor appoints a State Board of Education that also sets rules for local districts, approves texts, and has other assorted duties. Then there is the elected State Superintendent of Schools, who works with the State Board of Education and has jurisdiction over the State Department of Education. Honig, who was a political independent, worked with Republican governors (who appointed loyal party members to the State Board of Education) and Democratic legislatures. The opportunities for political mischief, if not antagonism, were abundant. Honig's resignation in 1992 can be attributed in part to the political conflicts over school reform. Ken Kelley, "The Interview: Bill Honig, Reading, Writing, and Reform," *San Francisco Focus,* June 1986, pp. 64–68; Bill Honig, *Last Chance for Our Children: How You Can Help Save Our Schools* (Reading, MA: Addison-Wesley, 1985).

26. Janet H. Crispeels, "Educational Policy Implementation in a Shifting Political Climate: The California Experience," *American Educational Research Journal* 34, no. 3 (1997): 453–481; Lisa Carlos and Mike Kirst, "California Curriculum Policy in the 1990s: We Don't Have To Be in Front To Lead," Policy Analysis for California Education and WestEd, 1997; Elaine Woo and Richard Colvin, "Lower Standards, Money, Changing Student Body Are the Challenges," *Los Angeles Times,* May 17, 1998, pp. S2–S8.

27. "Eastin Announces Statewide Plan for Education Technology: Connect, Compute, and Compete: C3," California Department of Education, News Release, #96–44, July 10, 1996.

28. Robert Johnston, "California," in "Technology Counts '99," *Education Week*, September 23, 1999, pp. 74–75.
29. Barnaby J. Feder, "Education Leads Silicon Valley Wish List," *New York Times*, January 22, 2001, p. C4.

2. CYBERTEACHING IN PRESCHOOLS AND KINDERGARTENS

1. All names of schools, teachers, and students are pseudonyms.
2. The research for this chapter was funded by Learning in the Real World and the Eco-Literacy Foundation in Berkeley, CA. Graduate students Lawrence Tovar and Huey Ru Lin collected and analyzed data at eleven Bay Area preschools and kindergartens. I wrote the final report, relying heavily upon the memos, summaries, and draft articles that they had written. In recognizing their contribution to this chapter, I will use the pronoun "we."
3. The Benjamin co-op, where parents are required to volunteer a minimal number of hours, is a district and state-funded preschool. It is also part of a federally funded technology project aimed at integrating the use of technology into daily teaching activities, particularly to help low-income children acquire early literacy skills. Rodrigues received machines, software, and technical support from the project.

   I visited Rodrigues's class four times over a two-year period. I also interviewed her once in addition to the two interviews that she gave to my research assistants. They observed her twice and interviewed children using the computer centers. Rodrigues also gave us a video of her teaching during "circle time," from which a portion of this vignette is drawn.
4. Erica Goode, "Mozart for Baby? Some Say, Maybe Not," *New York Times*, August 3, 1999, p. D1. The question comes from Lilian Katz and Sylvia Chard, *Engaging Children's Minds,* cited in Alison Armstrong and Charles Casement, *The Child and the Machine* (Toronto, Canada: Key Porter Books, 1998), p. 57.
5. Dean May and Maris Vinovskis, "A Ray of Millennial Light: Early Education and Social Reform in the Infant School Movement in Massachusetts, 1826–1840," in T. K. Hareven, ed., *Family and Kin in American Urban Communities, 1800–1940* (New York: Watts, 1977), pp. 62–99; Barbara Beatty, *Preschool Education in America: The Culture of Young Children from the Colonial Era to the Present* (New Haven: Yale University Press, 1995).
6. Beatty, *Preschool Education,* chs. 3–6.

7. Ibid., ch. 8; Greta Fein and Alison Clarke-Stewart, *Day Care in Context* (New York: John Wiley & Sons, 1973), pp. 13–25.

8. Beatty, *Preschool Education,* ch. 8; Mary Tabor, "Educators and the States Try To Shape Preschool," *New York Times,* June 17, 1998, p. A28; U.S. Bureau of the Census, *Current Population Reports,* series P-20, no. 443.

9. Scott Paris and Anne Cunningham, "Children Becoming Students," in David Berliner and Robert Calfee, eds., *Handbook of Educational Psychology* (New York: Macmillan Library Reference, 1996), pp. 123–128.

10. Quotations come from Joseph Tobin, David Y. H. Wu, and Dana Davidson, *Preschool in Three Cultures* (New Haven: Yale University Press, 1989), p. 173; Irving Sigel, "Early Childhood Education: Developmental Enhancement or Developmental Acceleration," in Sharon Kagan and Edward Zigler, eds., *Early Schooling: The National Debate* (New Haven: Yale University Press, 1987), pp. 129–150.

11. Lisbeth B. Schorr, *Within Our Reach: Breaking the Cycle of Disadvantage* (New York: Doubleday, 1988); Kathryn Kuntz, "Head Start's Origins in Community Action," in J. Ellsworth and L. Ames, *Critical Perspectives on Project Head Start* (Albany: State University of New York Press, 1998), pp. 1–48; Edward Zigler and Susan Muenchow, *Head Start: The Inside Story of America's Most Successful Educational Experiment* (New York: Basic Books, 1992); Maris Vinovskis, "School Readiness and Early Childhood Education," in Diane Ravitch and M. Vinovskis, eds., *Learning from the Past* (Baltimore: Johns Hopkins University Press, 1995).

12. Historically, political conservatives had challenged governmental funding of institutional childcare or early education on the grounds that the role of mothers was to care for young children. In 1987, for example, Senator Orrin Hatch (R, Utah), previously a strong opponent of day care, proposed a bill expanding both private and public day care programs. "I believe," he said, "that it is far preferable for parents to care for their own children, but I have been persuaded by the facts that our policy choice must be to enable citizens to work without fear for the safety and well-being of our children." Quoted in Tobin, Wu, and Davidson, *Preschool in Three Cultures,* p. 218.

13. Chris Pipho, "Kindergarten: One Size Doesn't Fit All!" *Education Week,* May 18, 1988, p. 25; Donna Bryant, Richard Clifford, and Ellen Peisner, "Best Practices for Beginners: Developmental Appropriateness in Kindergarten," *American Educational Research Journal* 28, no. 4 (1991):

783–803; Mary Lee Smith and Lorrie Shepard, "Kindergarten Readiness and Retention: A Qualitative Study of Teachers' Beliefs and Practices," *American Educational Research Journal* 25, no. 3 (1988): 307–333.

14. Jodi Wilgoren, "Toddling Off to Preschool," *New York Times,* October 31, 1999, p. 4; U.S. Department of Education, National Center for Education Statistics, ch. 2, Elementary and Secondary Education, table 49, http://nces.ed.gov/pubs99/digest98/d98t049.html; figures for enrollment of poor children come from ch. 2, p. 1, in http://www.acf.dhhs.gov/programs/hsreac/oct99/chapter2.htm; Jacqueline Salmon and Kirsten Grimsley, "States Expect Early Childhood Benefits," *Washington Post,* March 13, 2000, p. A5; U.S. Department of Education, "Participation in Education," *The Condition of Education 2000* (Washington, DC: National Center for Education Statistics, 2000), p. 7.

15. National Education Goals Panel, *The National Education Goals Report: Building a Nation of Learners, 1992* (Washington, DC: Government Printing Office, 1992), p. 58.

16. Sharon Noguchi, "The ABCs of Education Obsession," *San Jose Mercury News,* February 4, 2000, p. 6B; Katherine Corcoran, "Longer Days, Higher Standards Greet Kindergartners," *San Jose Mercury News,* September 6, 2000, p. 1.

17. Vinovskis, "School Readiness and Early Childhood Education," p. 260; Darcy Ann Olsen, "Universal Preschool Is No Golden Ticket," *Policy Analysis,* no. 333 (1999).

18. I have placed the word "good" in quotation marks to indicate that there is no one agreed-upon definition of a good school. There are many versions of good preschools and kindergartens or teachers, for that matter. See Larry Cuban, "Why Is It So Hard To Get Good Schools?" in Larry Cuban and Dorothy Shipps, eds., *Reconstructing the Common Good in Education: Coping with Intractable American Dilemmas* (Stanford: Stanford University Press, 2000).

19. I draw liberally from David Elkind, "Developmentally Appropriate Practice: A Case Study of Educational Inertia," in Sharon Kagan, ed., *The Care and Education of America's Young Children: Obstacles and Opportunities,* 90th Yearbook of National Society for the Study of Education (Chicago: NSSE, 1990), Part 1, pp. 1–17; Lilian Katz, "Pedagogical Issues in Early Childhood Education," ibid., pp. 50–68; Fein and Clarke-Stewart, *Day Care in Context,* pp. 199–207.

20. Fein and Clarke-Stewart, *Day Care in Context,* pp. 199–207; Abecedarian Project, http://www.fpg.unc.edu/~abc/executive_summary.htm.

21. We interviewed each teacher, parents, and at least two children in each classroom as they were using the computer. In the course of three visits to each school, we drew a classroom map, inventoried the various technologies in each classroom, observed students using computers, and interviewed both teachers and students.

22. The one site that didn't have a computer center was the Martes kindergarten. There were other types of activity centers, however. The teacher would schedule her class to go to the school's computer lab once a week for 30 minutes.

23. These levels are taken from Judith Sandholtz, Cathy Ringstaff, and David Dwyer, *Teaching with Technology* (New York: Teachers College Press, 1997), pp. 37–47.

24. National Association for Education of Young Children, "Position Statement: Technology and Young Children—Ages Three Through Eight," *Young Children* 51, no. 6 (1996): 11–21.

25. See Linda D. Labbo and David Reinking, "Negotiating the Multiple Realities of Technology in Literacy Research and Instruction," *Reading Research Quarterly* 34, no. 4 (1999): 478–492, for a summary of studies.

26. U.S. Department of Health and Human Services, Head Start Bureau, Memo on "Computers as an Early Childhood Learning Tool," ACYF-IM-90–19, June 36, 1990, p. 3.

27. *Head Start Bulletin: Nation Resources Exchange*, no. 19, January 1988. The four experts in order of reference above were Millie Almy, Barbara Bowman, Harriet Cuffaro, and Greta Fein.

28. Jane Healy, *Failure to Connect: How Computers Affect Our Children's Minds—for Better or Worse* (New York: Simon and Schuster, 1998), p. 205.

29. Ibid., pp. 203–218. Tic-tac-toe story cited in Healy, ibid., p. 207. Early childhood researchers and policymakers have a habit of citing brain research on infants and young children to support or rebut positions on the "critical period" of intellectual development. Most neuroscientists are reluctant to take what they know and apply that knowledge to preschool and kindergarten programs. See John Bruer, *The Myth of the First Three Years* (New York: Free Press, 1999).

30. David Elkind, "Young Children and Technology: A Cautionary Note," *Young Children* 51, no. 6 (1996): 22–23. Also see David Elkind, "Early Childhood Education on Its Own Terms," in Sharon Kagan and Edward Zigler, eds., *Early Schooling: The National Debate* (New Haven: Yale University Press, 1987), pp. 98–115.

31. Jerome Kagan, *Three Seductive Ideas* (Cambridge: Harvard University Press, 1998), pp. 83–88.

32. Douglas Clements, "Computers and Young Children: A Review of Research," *Young Children* 43, no. 1 (1987): 34–44.

33. John Bruer summarizes these views and how they have contributed to what he labels as "the myth" of accelerated intellectual development from birth through 3 years of age. He argues that few neuroscientists can say with confidence that results from studies warrant policies that push toddlers to read, write, and use computers as early as possible. See "Neural Connections: Some You Use, Some You Lose," *Kappan* 81, no. 4 (1999): 264–277. According to Alison Gopnik, Andrew Meltzoff, and Patricia Kuhl, we should be "deeply suspicious of any enterprise that offers a formula for making babies smarter or teaching them more, from flash cards to Mozart tapes to Better Baby Institutes. Everything we know about babies suggests that these artificial interventions are at best useless and at worst distractions from the normal interaction between grown-ups and babies." *The Scientists in the Crib* (New York: William Morrow, 2000), p. 201.

34. Douglas Clements, "Computers and Young Children: A Review of Research," *Young Children* 43, no. 1 (1987): 42.

35. Douglas Clements and Bonnie Nastasi, "Electronic Media and Early Childhood Education," in Bernard Spodek, ed., *Handbook of Research on the Education of Young Children* (New York: Macmillan, 1993), pp. 267–268.

36. Linda Labbo and Melanie Kuhn, "Weaving Chains of Affect and Cognition: A Young Child's Understanding of CD-ROM Talking Books," *Journal of Literacy Research* (in press).

37. National Association for Education of Young Children, "Position Statement" (1996).

38. For some young children who have disabilities or are educationally disadvantaged when they come to Head Start or kindergarten, using varied technologies to accommodate the diverse ways that both kinds of children learn has been shown to help these children acquire literacy and other skills. See Harvey Pressman and Peter Dublin, *Accommodating Learning Style Differences in Elementary Classrooms* (Fort Worth, TX: Harcourt Brace, 1995).

39. For the rationale to study early childhood classrooms and not the rest of elementary school experiences with computers, see the Appendix.

3. HIGH-TECH SCHOOLS, LOW-TECH LEARNING

1. All school, teacher, student, and administrator names are pseudonyms to protect the privacy of those who volunteered their time, ideas, and classrooms to our research team. All direct quotations come from interviews with teachers and direct observation of classrooms. The small-grants program of the Spencer Foundation funded the research for this chapter. Doctoral students Heather Kirkpatrick and Craig Peck worked together with me to collect and analyze data at the two high schools described in this chapter; they also contributed substantially to the final report. In addition we collaborated on an article of which Kirkpatrick and Peck wrote portions. This chapter includes excerpts from that article. As a result, I use "we" to acknowledge their contribution.

2. Claris Works is Apple software that includes art, drawing, database, and spreadsheet applications; AVID is a video-editing software program.

3. Henry Becker, Jason Ravitz, YanTien Wong, *Teaching, Learning, and Computing: 1998 National Survey* (Center for Research on Information Technology and Organizations, University of California, Irvine, and University of Minnesota, November 1999); Ronald Anderson and Amy Ronnkvist, "The Presence of Computers in American Schools," Report no. 2, *Teaching, Learning, and Computing: 1998 National Survey* (University of California, Irvine, June 1998).

4. Hugh Mehan, "Microcomputers in Classrooms: Educational Technology or Social Practice?" *Anthropology and Education Quarterly* 20 (1989): 4–22; Janet Schofield, *Computers and Classroom Culture* (London: Cambridge University Press, 1995); National Educational Assessment Program, *Math Assessment* (Princeton: Educational Testing Service, 1996).

5. Accurately determining teacher use of computers is difficult. Because machines and software are distributed in most schools between labs, libraries, and classrooms, statistics about access or figures showing how many students there are per computer within a school (25:1 or 6:1) are misleading if they are used to estimate either student or teacher use of the machines. Low ratios of students to computers in a school, say 3:1, is evidence of high access, but inferring high use by teachers and students is a leap of faith, not factual accuracy. Most statistics are derived from surveys of school officials and self-reports from teachers. Although such information is helpful, overestimates of use are common. Combining the few actual classroom studies with teacher and student reports of computer use offers increased reliability. Larry Cuban, *Teachers and Ma-*

chines (New York: Teachers College Press, 1986); Henry Becker, *School Uses of Microcomputers: Reports from a National Survey* (Baltimore: Johns Hopkins University, 1983); Henry Becker, "How Computers Are Used in United States Schools: Basic Data from the 1989 I.E.A. Computers in Education Survey," *Journal of Educational Computing Research* 7 (1991): 385–406; Henry Becker, "Analysis and Trends of School Use of New Information Technologies," Office of Technology Assessment (Washington, DC: U.S. Government Printing Office, 1996).

6. National Educational Assessment Program, *Reading Assessment* (Princeton: Educational Testing Service, 1994); National Educational Assessment Program, *Math Assessment* (Princeton: Educational Testing Service, 1996); National Center for Educational Statistics, *Condition of Education, 1997* (Washington, DC: U.S. Department of Education, 1997); Schofield, *Computers and Classroom Culture*; Barbara Means and Karen Olson, *Restructuring Schools with Technology* (Menlo Park: SRI International, 1995); U.S. Congress, Office of Technology Assistance, *Teachers and Technology* (Washington, DC: U.S. Government Printing Office, 1995); "Technology Counts," *Education Week*, November 10, 1997, pp. 17, 11.

In reviewing this section, Henry Becker challenged these figures as underestimates of use. In surveys that he and his colleagues conducted in 2000, elementary and middle school teachers reported far higher percentages of "occasional" use than I offer here. Becker gave me permission to cite his letter to Harvard University Press, which is in my possession.

7. Harold Wenglinsky, "Does It Compute? The Relationship between Educational Technology and Student Achievement in Mathematics," Policy Information Center, Research Division (Princeton: Educational Testing Service, 1998); National Educational Assessment Program, *Math Assessment* (Princeton: Educational Testing Service, 1996).

8. Over a seven-month period in 1998–1999, we visited two Silicon Valley comprehensive high schools known for acquiring and using new technologies. One high school enrolled about 1,900 students (with over 80 teachers) and the other, 1,300 students (with over 60 teachers). Between October 1998 and April 1999 we interviewed 21 teachers and 26 students in both schools who had volunteered to be part of our study. We surveyed two thirds to four fifths of both schools' faculties and one quarter to one third of each school's student body. We shadowed 12 students in both schools as they journeyed through a school day and did the same for 11 teachers at both schools. School staff provided us with teacher sign-up

data from both media centers and computer labs. Finally, we examined accreditation reports, proposals for launching reforms, grants seeking technology funds, and newspaper articles written about the schools.

9. The history of Las Montañas and the changes that have occurred since 1976 can be found in Beverly Carter, "The Limits of Control: Case Studies of High School Science Teachers Responses to State Curriculum Reform, 1981–1987," PhD diss., Stanford University, 1990, pp. 85–86, 94–96, 106–107; Western Association of Schools and Colleges Self-Study, 1993–1994; Western Association of Schools and Colleges, Self-Study Report, "Focus on Learning," 1996–1997.

10. WASC, "Focus on Learning, 1996–1997," p. 24.

11. History of principals is drawn from interviews with teachers and administrators and two accreditation reports (1993 and 1996). Figures for enrollment in interdisciplinary programs come from application for Bay Area School Reform Collaborative (BASRC), p. 33.

12. Interview with one of the two remaining teachers. Quotation is taken from application to BASRC, p. 30.

13. BASRC Report, February 1, 1999; Digital High School Grant application, March 1999.

14. Data for Flatland comes from its "School Accountability Report Card 1996–1997," from www.greatschools.net, and from a grant application to Sun Microsystems, December 1998.

15. Interview with principal, March 19, 1999.

16. Memo from assistant principal to Cuban on ninth grade restructuring, June 10, 1999; grant proposal to local firm for 30 Java stations, December 1998.

17. "Pursuing Excellence: WASC Accreditation Study, 1990–1991"; "Pursuing Excellence: WASC/State Department of Education 3 Year On Site Review, 1993–1994"; WASC Site Visit, "Focus on Learning," April 1997.

18. "Technology Counts," *Education Week*, November 10, 1997, p. 8; ibid., October 1, 1998, p. 103; ibid., September 23, 1999, p. 64. Cost estimates of both hardware and software vary. Cost of current hardware in schools (as of 1996) is about $3 billion. To deploy computers into one 25-PC networked lab in each school would cost $11 billion; for a networked PC for every five students, the estimated cost would be $47 billion (ETS, 1997, p. 5).

19. "Technology Counts," *Education Week*, September 23, 1999, p. 64.

20. Ibid., November 10, 1997.

21. Judith Sandholtz, Cathy Ringstaff, and David Dwyer, *Teaching with Technology* (New York: Teachers College Press, 1997), pp. 37–47.

22. This section on open-door and tech-god students is taken from an article by Craig Peck, Larry Cuban, and Heather Kirkpatrick, "Techno-Promoter Dreams, Student Realities," *Kappan* (forthcoming).

23. Nationally, 30 percent of schools have a full-time tech coordinator, 27 percent have a teacher or other staff performing some of these duties, 20 percent has district staff, and 10 percent have a part-time coordinator for tech support. The remaining percentage included volunteers, contracted tech support, and 2 percent of the schools that have no coordinator or volunteer. "Technology Counts," 1999, p. 61.

24. We determined the estimate by combining the handful of students that teachers identified as tech gods and open-door students with the enrollment totals in tech-based electives and academic courses with serious technology-using teachers.

25. Seymour Sarason, *The Culture of the School and the Problem of Change* (Boston: Allyn and Bacon, 1971); John Goodlad, *A Place Called School* (New York: McGraw-Hill, 1984); Susan Rosenholtz, *Teachers' Workplace: The Social Organization of Schools* (New York: Longman, 1989); David Cohen, "Teaching Practice, Plus Que Ca Change . . . ," in P. Jackson, ed., *Contributing to Educational Change: Perspective on Research and Practice* (Berkeley: McCutchan, 1988): pp. 27–84.

26. For examples of writers who have claimed that a revolution in teaching and learning will occur as a result of information technologies penetrating public schools, see Seymour Papert, *The Children's Machine: Rethinking School in the Age of the Computer* (New York: Basic Books, 1993); Marvin Cetron and Margaret Gayle, *Educational Renaissance: Our Schools at the Turn of the Twenty-First Century* (New York: St. Martin's Press, 1996); Ronald Thorpe, "Can Computers Change the System?" *Education Week*, October 20, 1999, http://www.edweek.org/ewstory.cfm?slug=08thorpe.h19&. Also see standards for the use of technology in schools published by the International Society for Technology in Education (ISTE), 1999 at http://cnets.iste.org.

27. The distinction we draw between incremental and fundamental changes in teaching practice and school reform are described and analyzed in Larry Cuban, *How Teachers Taught* (New York: Teachers College Press, 1993), and in Larry Cuban, *How Scholars Trumped Teachers: Change without Reform in University Curriculum, Research, and Teaching, 1890–1990* (New York: Teachers College Press, 1999).

28. Careful readers may object at this point to these statements about maximal access and minimal change. Most classrooms in both schools had

only one computer and teachers had to take their classes to the media center or an available lab (except for those teachers in the business and computer departments, which had rooms with 25—30 machines). In these schools, the classroom is hardly a technology-rich environment. Thus, the school may have been abundantly outfitted with new technologies for instruction but the classroom had meager access. Such limited access may well account for the kinds of instruction we observed.

Perhaps. Other data need to be kept in mind about teacher and student access to classroom and school computers for instruction. First, there were two classrooms at Flatland (biology and history) and two at Las Montañas (English and social studies) that had six to eight computers in each room available to students and teacher daily. Also at Las Montañas, there was a mobile cart with four to six computers that teachers could (and many did) bring to their rooms. We observed classes in these rooms and found that teachers directed some students to use the computers a few times a week for particular activities. In most instances, these activities were word processing and Internet searches. In other words, the familiar teacher-centered patterns we observed in other classrooms and the limited use of the machines *suggest*–and that is the strongest word we can use, given the limited number of classrooms we saw— that multiple computers in a classroom had not led to many alterations in teaching practices.

Also, at the school level where labs and the media center provided access to computers for instruction, we found that both media centers and labs for which we had data were not booked the entire school day. There were times each day that we observed, and have data for, when the lab was empty. Our estimate is that at least one third of the time that computers were available in these locations, the labs went unused. And as we have already suggested, when the labs and media centers *were* used, except for the few teachers we have identified in each high school, more often than not students used the machines for word processing and Internet searches. Although our data are partial and suggest that the overall patterns we noted would not have changed were there more computers in each class, other studies of high school teachers and student use would need to be done where access to computers is in the four to six range per classroom to determine whether the patterns we noted in these two high schools were unique.

29. Lists of obstacles, constraints, and problems to overcome in teacher use of computers appear commonly in books, articles, and exhortations by advocates of placing more machines in schools and classrooms. See, for

example, U.S. Congress, Office of Technology Assessment, *Teachers and Technology: Making the Connection,* OTA-EHR-616 (Washington, DC: U.S. Government Printing Office, 1995), pp. 129–130; President's Committee of Advisors on Science and Technology, *Report to the President on the Use of Technology to Strengthen K-12 Education in the United States* (1997), pp. 113–122. Age, gender, and teacher resistance as explanatory factors are seldom made explicit in current policy debates, probably because of concerns over causing additional resistance. But in our discussions with teachers, students, administrators, and policymakers, statements about older teachers being too rigid, women being nontechnical, and teachers fearing job loss and retirement, or becoming closet Luddites, were heard often enough to be noticeable. We found no evidence of teacher resistance; in fact, we noted repeatedly, both in word and deed, enthusiasm for home and school use for class preparation, communication, and administrative tasks. We also noted that female and male teachers owned computers in roughly equal proportions and that many older teachers in the schools were both serious and occasional users.

4. NEW TECHNOLOGIES IN OLD UNIVERSITIES

1. Interview with Sue Crawford, former head of facilities at the School of Education. Also her memo to me about SCRDT, June 30, 1992. I informally interviewed colleagues in the School of Education who were part of SCRDT.
2. *Chronicle of Higher Education,* June 16, 1993, pp. A2–3.
3. Thomas Deloughry, "Studio Classrooms," *Chronicle of Higher Education,* March 31, 1995, pp. A19–21.
4. Thomas Friedman, "Next, It's E-ducation," *New York Times,* November 17, 1999, p. A29.
5. "For the Record: Faculty Senate Report," *Stanford Report,* February 9, 2000, p. 12.
6. Stukel quotation in "Teaching at an Internet Distance: The Pedagogy of Online Teaching and Learning. The Report of a 1998–1999 University of Illinois Faculty Seminar," http//:www.vpaa.uillinois.edu/tid/report/tid_report.html; William Massy and Robert Zemsky, *Using Information Technology to Enhance Academic Productivity* (Washington, DC: EDUCOM, 1995), pp. 1–2. William Massy, an economist, served as a top administrator at Stanford.
7. Peter Applebome, "The On-Line Revolution Is Not the End of Civiliza-

tion as We Know It. But Almost," *New York Times,* Education Supplement, April 4, 1999, pp. 26–28, 35–37; Goldie Blumenstyk, "Some Elite Private Universities Get Serious about Distance Learning," *Chronicle of Higher Education,* June 20, 1997, pp. A23–24; Jody Wilgoren, "A Revolution Clicks into Place," *New York Times,* March 26, 2000, pp. 1, 27. For a dissenting view of online courses, see David Noble's series on "Digital Diploma Mills" (http://www.communication.UCSD.edu/dl/).

8. William Geoghegan, "Whatever Happened to Instructional Technology," report from IBM Academic Consulting and from Proceedings of the 22nd Annual Conference of the International Business Schools Computing Association, July 17–20, 1994, pp. 1–2; K. C. Green and S. Eastman, *Campus Computing 1993: The USC National Survey of Desktop Computing in Higher Education* (Los Angeles: University of Southern California, 1994); "1999 Higher Education Technology Findings," December 1999 in http://www.schooldata.com/datapoint43.html; Florence Olsen, "Many Colleges Are in a Spending Spree for Information Technology," *Chronicle of Higher Education,* March 3, 2000, p. A52.

9. Kenneth Green, *Campus Computing, 1995: The Sixth National Survey of Desktop Computing in Higher Education* (Encino, CA: Campus Computing, 1996); Green and Eastman, *Campus Computing 1993;* J. M. Shanks, "Faculty Computing in the University of California: Rationale, Design, and Summary Results for the 1992 Survey on Instructional Use of Computers," Presentation at EDUCOM '93, Cincinnati, Ohio October 19, 1993; Thomas DeLoughry, "Survey of Language Professors Finds Extensive Use of Computers," *Chronicle of Higher Education,* April 21, 1993, pp. A27, 32.

10. Thomas Deloughry, "Studio Classrooms," *Chronicle of Higher Education,* March 31, 1995, pp. A19–21. Ben Shneiderman, Elen Yu Borkowski, Maryam Alavi, and Kent Norman, "Emergent Patterns of Teaching/Learning in Electronic Classrooms," *Educational Technology Research & Development* 46, no. 4 (1998): 23–42; the estimate of early adopters comes from Robert Kozma and Jerome Johnston, "The Technological Revolution Comes to the Classroom," *Change,* January/February 1991, p. 10; http://stanford.edu/dept/news/pr/96/960124beanbag.html; Everett Rogers, *The Diffusion of Innovations,* 3rd ed. (New York: Free Press, 1983). Rogers acknowledges that "laggards" is a negative term but uses it to describe tradition-bound people who look to the past and have little influence in the organization. See p. 250. Rogers does not examine the premise that innovations are inherently good and should be adopted by all in a system.

11. Wagner Thielens, Jr., "The Disciplines and Undergraduate Lecturing," paper presented at the annual meeting of the American Educational Research Association, Washington, DC, April 1987; also see Robert Blackburn, Glenn Pellino, Alice Boberg, and Colman O'Connell, "Are Instructional Programs Off-Target," Project for Faculty Development Program Evaluation (Ann Arbor: University of Michigan, Center for the Study of Higher Education, 1980), pp. 32–48; Educational Testing Service, *Student Instructional Report: Comparative Data Guide for Four-Year Colleges and Universities* (1979). For histories that describe teaching methods in universities see Laurence Veysey, *The Emergence of the American University* (Chicago: University of Chicago Press, 1965); Larry Cuban, *How Scholars Trumped Teachers: Change without Reform in University Curriculum, Research, and Teaching, 1890–1990* (New York: Teachers College Press, 1999).

12. Mark Shields, "The Legitimation of Academic Computing in the 1980s," in Mark Shields, *Work and Technology in Higher Education* (Hillsdale, NJ: Erlbaum, 1995), pp. 161–187; Sara Kiesler and Lee Sproull, eds. *Computing and Change on Campus* (New York: Cambridge University Press, 1987).

13. For a clear example of unanticipated outcomes in using computers for instruction, see Patrick McQuillan, "Computers and Pedagogy: The Invisible Presence," in Shields, *Work and Technology*, pp. 103–129.

14. The label "Research I and II" comes from a Carnegie-funded taxonomy of higher education institutions. See Carnegie Foundation for the Advancement of Teaching, *A Classification of Higher Education* (1987), pp. 3–4, 7–8. The classification scheme was changed in 1994 and the number of Research I and II institutions increased from 104 to 125. See Jean Evangelauf, "A New 'Carnegie Classification,'" *Chronicle of Higher Education,* April 6, 1994, pp. A17–26; Roger Geiger, *To Advance Knowledge: The Growth of American Research Universities* (New York: Oxford University Press, 1986); Clark Kerr, *Troubled Times for American Higher Education: The 1990s and Beyond* (New York: SUNY Press, 1993).

15. Julie Reuben, *The Making of the Modern University* (Chicago: University of Chicago Press, 1996), pp. 61–87; Mary Ann Dzuback, *Robert M. Hutchins: Portrait of an Educator* (Chicago: University of Chicago Press, 1991), pp. 109–135; Daniel Bell, *The Reforming of General Education* (New York: Columbia University Press, 1966), pp. 12–68; Richard Freeland, *Academy's Golden Age: Universities in Massachusetts, 1945–1990* (New York: Oxford University Press, 1992), pp. 123–130.

16. Joseph Ben-David, *American Higher Education* (1972), pp. 87–109; Patti

Gumport, "Graduate Education and Research Imperatives," in B. Clark, ed., *The Research Foundations of Graduate Education: Germany, Britain, France, United States, Japan* (Berkeley: University of California Press, 1993), pp. 261–293; Hugh Hawkins, "University Identity: The Teaching and Research Function," in A. Oleson and J. Voss, eds., *The Organization of Knowledge in Modern America, 1860–1920* (Baltimore: Johns Hopkins University Press, 1979), pp. 285–312.

17. Historians and social scientists Geiger, Veysey, Clark, Kerr, and Reuben studied groups of research-oriented universities that included Stanford as one of their cases. Many historians have drawn from Stanford's archives. W. B. Carnochan has written about the long-term curricular struggle over a liberal education (with little mention of the accompanying pedagogy) in *The Battleground of the Curriculum* (Stanford: Stanford University Press, 1993). Rebecca Lowen concentrated upon Stanford after World War II and its rise to prominence. Using the papers of Provost Frederick Terman and President Wallace Sterling, Lowen argued that the transformation of Stanford came largely as a result of administrative initiatives in securing federal and private funding during and after World War II. See *Creating the Cold War University* (Berkeley: University of California Press, 1997). For Stanford's rise in national prestige, see Cuban, *How Scholars Trumped Teachers*, ch. 1.

18. David Kaplan, *The Silicon Boys* (New York: William Morrow, 1999), pp. 31–34, 37, 283–284, 312; Michael Lewis, *The New New Thing* (New York: W. W. Norton, 1999), pp. 39–40; Rebecca Lowen, *Creating the Cold War University* (Berkeley: University of California Press, 1997).

19. The Stanford University Board of Trustees appointed Provost John Hennessy President of Stanford in April 2000. A professor of electrical Engineering at Stanford and later dean of the School of Engineering, Hennessy wrote an important textbook on designing computers and founded a semiconductor company. Evelyn Nieves, "Computer Scientist Picked as President of Stanford," *New York Times*, April 4, 2000, p. A10. For faculty and student figures, see www.stanford.edu/home/stanford facts/faculty.html and www.stanford.edu/home/stanford/facts/graduate.html; Casper quoted in *Speaking of Computers*, no. 45, September 22, 1997, p. 1.

20. For the early history of computing at Stanford, I draw heavily on two unpublished doctoral dissertations completed at Stanford: Jacqueline Ann Schmidt-Posner, "Electronic Ivory Towers: Organizational Approaches to Faculty Microcomputers" (1989), and Debbie Leong-Childs, "Professors'

Use of Computers for Innovative Instruction" (1989). The quotation is from Schmidt-Posner, p. 45.

21. Professor Pat Suppes cited in Schmidt-Posner, "Electronic Ivory Towers," p. 83.

22. Administrator cited in Leong-Childs, "Professors' Use of Computers," pp. 83–84.

23. Ibid., p. 99.

24. *Speaking of Computers*, no. 39, September 25, 1995, pp. 1, 5–6, 13; ibid., no. 43, January 20, 1997, pp. 1–3, 8–10; ibid., no. 45, September 22, 1997, pp. 1–4. Information on available technologies is described in http://acomp.stanford.edu/. Additional information on computer clusters came from David Hsu at Stanford Libraries, October 26, 1999; *Speaking of Computers*, no. 54, September 25, 2000, p. 6.

25. Many more faculty and student services offered in academic computing go unelaborated here. For example, there has been a large degree-offering distance-learning program aimed at employees in business and engineering. The Learning Lab and Center of Innovation recently have been established to evaluate instructional technology in teaching and learning and cultivate additional projects that aim to improve instruction. See *Speaking of Computers*, no. 45, September 22, 1997, pp. 1–2; http://acomp.stanford.edu/atss/atl/; Deborah Kong, "Stanford Offers Courses through Virtual Campus," *San Jose Mercury News*, September 9, 1995, pp. 1B, 6B; Elaine Ray, "Wallenberg Gift to Help Stanford to 'Re-Imagine Itself'" *Stanford Report*, March 10, 1999, pp. 1, 6–7.

26. *Stanford*, November/December 1996, p. 19; *Speaking of Computers*, no. 54, September 25, 2000, p. 1. Kathleen O'Toole, "Learning Curves Slowing Scholars on Info Highway," *Campus Report*, November 9, 1994, p. 9; Committee on Academic Computing Report, *Campus Report*, June 7, 1989, pp. 20–22; unpublished "Faculty Survey of Technology Use," August 1997, Question 91.

27. Cuban, *How Scholars Trumped Teachers*, pp. 37, 46.

28. *The Study of Education at Stanford*, vol. 2, "Undergraduate Curriculum," pp. 56–58. The response rate to the survey by graduating seniors was 53 percent.

29. "Report of the Subcommittee on Techniques and Technology in Teaching and Learning," May 9, 1994, n.p. See answers to question 26. There was a 35 percent response rate to the survey.

30. Nira Hativa, "What Are the Cultures of Teaching of University Profes-

sors: Results of a Survey for Stanford Professors," unpublished report, July 1995, pp. 31–32. Response rate to this survey was 20 percent.

31. Diane Manuel and Marisa Cigarroa, "Casper Adds Millions for Professorships and Fellowships," *Stanford Report,* May 10, 1996, p. 6.

32. "Who's the Teacher," *Stanford Daily,* January 8, 1997, p. 4.

33. For a description of the Prospective Principals Program and the form of problem-based learning employed within it, see Edwin M. Bridges, *Implementing Problem Based Learning in Leadership Development* (Eugene, OR: ERIC Clearinghouse on Educational Management, University of Oregon, 1995). Hugh Skilling in the Engineering School edited an unusual collection of essays, *Do You Teach? Views on College Teaching* (New York: Holt, Rinehart & Winston, 1969). I have attended classes in the Law, Business and Engineering schools.

34. I draw this section from my earlier study, *How Scholars Trumped Teachers.*

35. Hativa, "What Are the Cultures of Teaching of University Professors"; Stanford University, *Report of Commission on Undergraduate Education, 1994*; Survey results are in the appendix. Eric Dey, Claudia E. Ramirez, William Korn, and Alexander Astin, *The American College Teacher: National Norms for the 1992–1993 HERI Faculty Survey* (Los Angeles: Higher Education Research Institute, 1993). One difference needs to be noted. The use of instructional technologies has been far more advanced in the preclinical sciences than in the teaching of history. Much anatomy instruction has been enhanced by interactive software and videos since the late 1970s. Students also had access to lectures on video for certain courses. Slides were shown routinely in lectures. See Laurel Joyce, "Medical Education's Brave New World," *Stanford Medicine* 8, no. 3 (1991): 4–9. In the History Department, a few professors have created specific software programs for particular topics in certain courses. But most professors, at least in the early-1990s, had continued to use conventional means of teaching. "The slowness that [technology] penetrates this environment," historian David Kennedy noted, "is really quite remarkable." Interview with Kennedy, July 22, 1996.

36. Hativa, "What Are the Cultures of Teaching of University Professors"; Dey, Ramirez, Korn, and Astin, *The American College Teacher,* p. 15.

37. The evidence for these statements is fragmentary and largely drawn from doctoral dissertations, Stanford faculty surveys, and interviews cited in chapters 1–4 of *How Scholars Trumped Teachers.* Thus they are closer to inferences than factual statements. Moreover, teaching practices vary

across departments and professional schools. Further strengthening the inference about beliefs concerning teaching and the importance of subject matter has been the historic absence of preparatory programs in teaching for those who seek to become academics. These pervasive beliefs about the role of teaching seem to be shared by other academics in universities across the nation. See Burton R. Clark, *The Academic Life: Small Worlds, Different Worlds* (Princeton: Carnegie Foundation for the Advancement of Teaching, 1987), pp. 123–125.

38. Robin Wilson, "A Decade of Teaching 'Reform Calculus' Has Been a Disaster, Critics Charge," *Chronicle of Higher Education,* February 7, 1997, pp. 1, 16. Such innovations have split departments. At Stanford, the math department began to teach calculus using different materials and methods and then abandoned the innovation after a few years. Ralph Cohen returned to the traditional format, saying: "For students who really need to know math and use it, this wasn't nearly sophisticated or rigorous enough." To Professor Brad Osgood, one of the advocates for teaching "reform calculus," the debate over how to teach the subject and the return to the traditional format has left him so isolated that he joined another department. Ibid. Also see essays by Howard Aldrich, Darlene Bailey, and Karl Weick on their celebration of teaching in Rae Andre and Peter Frost, eds, *Researchers Hooked on Teaching* (Thousand Oaks, CA: Sage, 1997).

39. "Student Orientation Packet, PCM-C, Spring 1994"; Terry Blaschke, Course Director; in the Stanford Law School and Graduate School of Business the case-method, as at other universities, is a staple in professors' repertoires; Kelly Skeff and Nell Noddings, *Teaching Improvement in the University* (Stanford: Stanford University Press, 1985). For the range of beliefs on subject matter and process of teaching, see Katherine Samuelowicz and John D. Bain, "Conceptions of Teaching Held by Academic Teachers," *Higher Education* 24 (1992): 93–111.

40. See student evaluations of David Potter's teaching in SC88, folder 10; for various courses taught by David Kennedy, see Stanford students "Course Review" for 1973, 1978, 1979. Kennedy also received the Dean's Award for Outstanding Teaching twice.

41. Leong-Childs constructed the survey for a randomly chosen list of 150 professors from Humanities and Sciences divided evenly into humanists, natural scientists, and social scientists. Amazingly, she achieved an 80 percent return; most faculty surveys yield a 25–35 percent response rate. Pp. 233–234.

42. The Faculty Senate charged the Committee on Academic Computing in July 1988 to prepare a report on computer use "in those parts of the academic community traditionally not accustomed to using computers." The committee designed a questionnaire and sent it in April 1989 to 662 faculty members in the humanities, with comparison groups being drawn from natural scientists and social scientists. Approximately 45 percent of the faculty returned the survey. *Campus Report,* June 7, 1989, pp. 20–21.

43. Commission on Undergraduate Education, "Report of the Subcommittee on Techniques and Technology in Teaching and Learning," May 9, 1994. The response rate from faculty was 35 percent.

44. Email (October 27, 1999) from Thomas Hier, a consultant who collected data for this survey; data came from the Office of the Registrar from which surveys were distributed in August 1997. These results are in my possession.

45. For 1989 survey, see p. 22 of *Campus Report.* In 1994 survey 66 percent of faculty said that the lack of time was a strong factor in developing software; for 45 percent of responding professors, the lack of time to simply learn about new technologies was a strong factor in their decision about use. For 1997 survey, Question 35 asked faculty to rank reasons for not being interested in computer-based classroom technologies, 81 percent of the faculty who responded said that having "support" was "very" to "moderately important."

46. The Office of the Registrar did not have data for the third classroom. Sign-up data for the other two classrooms were on the Web.

47. The discrepancy between 47 faculty and 42 with identified rank is due to five faculty listed in the schedule with no name attached. I could not identify their rank but I could identify their departments.

48. The sign-up schedules for the three years were available on the Web. I counted every course and faculty member who had signed up for the hours listed for the months of October through June. I did not include September because classes usually began the last week of that month. Heather Reid, who oversees the scheduling, provided additional information on these classes.

49. There are a few exceptions to the generally positive articles that appear in the print and video media. See, for example, a story about Richard Zare, a Stanford University chemistry professor who hired a consultant to straighten out his email. The article inventories the difficulties of the new technologies and their unfriendliness to users. Tia O'Brien, "Be-glitched, Bothered, and Bewildered," *West,* October 22, 1995, pp. 8–13, 26.

50. *Speaking of Computers,* no. 41, April 15, 1996, p. 11.
51. Marisa Cigarroa, "E-Mail, Web Sites: No More Pencils, No More Books?" *Campus Report,* September 13, 1995, p. 7.
52. Notes of interview by Avis Austin of Stephen Boyd, November 3, 1995.
53. Cigarroa, "E-Mail, Web Sites," p. 7.
54. In 1997, one organization specifically charged with researching and evaluating the impact of technology on teaching and learning is the Learning Lab. The staff has investigated classroom uses of technology. One project has been to evaluate the use of a tool for managing online discussion groups in large lecture courses. For two quarters in 1998–1999, 32 instructors in the same Humanities introductory course used the software called *Forum.* The staff of the Learning Lab has used interviews, focus groups, and surveys of students to determine how *Forum* affected learning. In another project, Learning Lab staff assessed the worth of students having to submit problem-sets for an introductory course in Human Biology over the World Wide Web. The computer system would grade student answers. Students would then return to the Web site to see explanations of the correct answers, review their responses, and pick up their scores. Results from both projects showed modest positive impact on learning and communication between and among students and professors. See: http//learninglab.stanford.edu.
55. Jacqueline Schmidt-Posner, "Electronic Ivory Towers," documents a similar variation in the early 1980s in her examination of the Law School, School of Education, and Graduate School of Business.
56. See the Law School's site map and courses taught by John Barton and Margaret Radin (http://www.law.stanford.edu).
57. See http://www-med.stanford.edu.
58. See Cuban, *How Scholars Trumped Teachers,* pp. 150–153.
59. See http://summit.stanford.edu. Click on "Curricular Projects." See Cuban, *How Scholars Trumped Teachers,* p. 161.
60. See http://stanford-online.stanford.edu/help/section1.html.

5. MAKING SENSE OF UNEXPECTED OUTCOMES

1. Edward Tenner, *Why Things Bite Back* (New York: Knopf, 1997), pp. 150–160.
2. Debbie Bookchin and Jim Schumacher, "The Virus and the Vaccine," *Atlantic Monthly* 285, no. 2 (2000): 68–80; "Revenge effects" was coined by Tenner, *Why Things Bite Back,* pp. 7–13.

3. Robert Merton, "The Unanticipated Consequences of Purposive Social Action," in Robert Merton, *Sociological Ambivalence and Other Essays* (New York: Free Press, 1976), pp. 145–155. I argue that repeated appearances of the same "unanticipated consequences" from earlier reform effects during and after a new school reform suggests that reformers are forgetful and have had, at worst, a cavalier attitude toward earlier and similar reforms. Such instances of unanticipated results would be different from what aircraft designers call "unk-unks," the unknown-unknowns, or problems that could not be anticipated because the engineers did not even know they existed. See Robert Thomas, *What Machines Can't Do* (Berkeley: University of California Press, 1994), p. 149.

4. Merton, "Unanticipated Consequences," p. 146; David Tyack and Elisabeth Hansot, *Learning Together* (New Haven: Yale University Press, 1990); Albert Hirschman, *The Rhetoric of Reaction: Perversity, Futility, and Jeopardy* (Cambridge: Harvard University Press, 1991).

5. When I use the word "teacher" I refer to preschool, K–12, and higher education practitioners, including professors. Occasionally, I will refer to teachers at a particular level as exceptions.

6. An exception to this statement is the preschool and kindergarten teachers that we observed and interviewed, primarily because we chose only those volunteers who had identified themselves as computer-using teachers, although their use may range from occasional to serious. Henry Becker challenged my claim of abundant access to new technologies, particularly in the two Silicon Valley high schools, where each classroom had only one computer but many labs and a media center in each one. His point is that classroom availability, say four to six computers, is the more relevant standard than schoolwide access, the standard that I used. How, he asks, can you expect teachers to use computers often when they only have one in their classrooms? There is support for Becker's point in his 1998 survey and one completed in 1999 by the National Center of Educational Statistics. In both surveys, secondary academic teachers who had five to eight computers in their classrooms reported they used the technology for instruction more often than colleagues with one or two machines. Classroom availability in academic subjects, Becker argues, leads to more use than schoolwide availability in labs and media centers. He may well be correct. In our two schools, however, when we observed academic classrooms with six to ten computers, the evidence was, at best, mixed—hardly supporting the two surveys containing teacher self-reports. See http://www.crito.uci.edu/tlc/findings/report4 and National Center for Education Statistics, "Teachers' Tools for the 21st Century," September

2000, NCES 2000–102 (Washington, DC: U.S. Department of Education, Office of Educational Research and Improvement, 2000), pp. 59–60.

7. See Larry Cuban, *How Teachers Taught* (New York: Teachers College Press, 1993).

8. Larry Cuban, *Teachers and Machines: The Classroom Use of Technology since 1920* (New York: Teachers College Press, 1986). I concentrated on K–12 teachers.

9. Ibid., pp. 27–36.

10. Ibid., pp. 16–17, 24, 39–41.

11. Ibid., pp. 66–69. For description of mainstream practices of teachers between 1890–1980, see Cuban, *How Teachers Taught*, chs. 5–6; John I. Goodlad, *A Place Called School* (New York: McGraw-Hill, 1984).

12. Donald Norman, *The Invisible Computer* (Cambridge: MIT Press, 1998), pp. 168–169.

13. The categories of adopters come from Everett Rogers, *Diffusion of Innovations*, 4th ed. (New York: Free Press, 1995), p. 247.

14. See Rogers for "S" curve in ibid., pp. 243–251. Also see Gene Rochlin, *Trapped in the Net: The Unanticipated Consequences of Computerization* (Princeton: Princeton University Press, 1997), chs. 4, 6–8, for descriptions of new technologies for managers, corporate traders, commercial pilots, and military officers. Rochlin also summarizes the few studies done on nuclear reactors.

15. I have drawn this section from the following studies: Tracy Kidder, *The Soul of a New Machine* (New York: Avon Books, 1981); Thomas, *What Machines Can't Do*; Robert Zussman, *Mechanics of the Middle Class* (Berkeley: University of California Press, 1985); Kathryn Henderson, *On Line and On Paper: Visual Representations, Visual Culture, and Computer Graphics in Design Engineering* (Cambridge: MIT Press, 1999); Leslie Perlow, *Finding Time: How Corporations, Individuals, and Families Can Benefit from New Work Practices* (Ithaca: IRL Press, 1997); Louis Bucciarelli, *Designing Engineers* (Cambridge: MIT Press, 1994).

16. Thomas, *What Machines Can't Do*, pp. 65–75; Bucciarelli, *Designing Engineers*, pp. 29–36, 165–179.

17. Henderson, *On Line and On Paper*, p. 160.

18. Ibid., p. 83.

19. See http://www.skunkworks.net/company_overview.html.

20. Kidder, *Soul of a New Machine*.

21. Thomas, *What Machines Can't Do*, p. 50.

22. Henderson, *On Line and On Paper*, pp. 98–99.

23. Evidence-based Medicine Working Group, "Evidence-Based Medicine: A New Approach to Teaching the Practice of Medicine, *Journal of American Medical Association* 266, no. 17 (1992): 2420–2425.

24. Allen Shaughnessy, David Slawson, and Lorne Becker, "Clinical Jazz: Harmonizing Clinical Experience and Evidence-Based Medicine," *Journal of Family Practice* 47, no. 6 (1998): 426.

25. David Sackett, Letter to the Editor, *Lancet* 346 (1995): 840. Elsewhere, Sackett has defined EBM as the "conscientious, explicit, and judicious use of current best evidence in making decisions about the care of individual patients." David Sackett, William Rosenberg, J. A. Gray, R. B. Haynes, and W. S. Richardson, "Evidence-Based Medicine: What It Is and What It Isn't," *British Medical Journal* 312 (1996): 71–72.

26. Martin Dawes, "On the Need for Evidence-Based General and Family Practice," *Evidence-Based Medicine* 1, no. 3 (1996): 68–69; Sharon Straus, "Bringing Evidence to the Point of Care," *Evidence-Based Medicine* 4 (1999): 70–71.

27. *Newsweek*, September 20, 1999, http://www.newsweek.com/nw-srv/printed/us/st/sr1212_2.htm.

28. Jeremy Anderson, Elizabeth Burrows, Paul Fennessy, and Sue Shaw, "An 'Evidence Centre' in a General Hospital," *Evidence-based Medicine* 4 (1999): 102–103. Dawes, "On the Need for Evidence-based General and Family Practice," p. 70.

29. D. G. Covell, G. C. Uman, P. R. Manning, "Information Needs in Office Practice: Are They Being Met?" *Annals of Internal Medicine* 10 (1985): 596–599; S. P. Curley, D. P. Connelly, and E. C. Rich, "Physicians' Use of Medical Knowledge Resources," *Medical Decision Making* 10 (1990): 231–241. Both are cited in Paul Gorman and Mark Helfand, "Information Seeking in Primary Care: How Physicians Choose Which Clinical Questions to Pursue and Which to Leave Unanswered," *Medical Decision Making* 15, no. 2 (1995): 113–119.

30. Gorman and Helfand, "Information Seeking in Primary Care," p. 116.

31. James Lenhart, Karen Honess, Deborah Covington, and Kevin Johnson, "An Analysis of Trends, Perceptions, and Use Patterns of Electronic Medical Records among U.S. Family Practice Residency Programs," *Family Medicine* 32, no. 2 (2000): 109–114. There was a respectable 72 percent return for the survey.

32. Ibid., pp. 113–114.

33. To capture the intractable uncertainties that accompany medical practice even with the most astute specialists who use every study at their command, see Jerome Groopman, "Second Opinion," *New Yorker* 75, no. 43

(1999): 40–49. Groopman ends the article about a serious division of opinion with a colleague over whether a patient should have a bone marrow transplant by saying: "This was medicine, not physics . . . human biology is too variable to be reduced to mathematical calculation. Intuition would still count, and so would luck," p. 49.

34. That inventions, which spread rapidly through an occupation or even society, are often grafted onto traditional practices is familiar. In Carolyn Marvin's study of the spread of electrical lighting and communication in the nineteenth century, she concluded that "early uses of technological innovations are essentially conservative because their capacity to create social disequilibrium is intuitively recognized amidst declarations of progress and enthusiasm for the new . . . The past really does survive in the future." *When Old Technologies Were New* (New York: Oxford University Press, 1988), p. 235.

35. The idea of incremental changes accumulating into revolutionary or fundamental transformations can be found in Larry Cuban, *How Scholars Trumped Teachers* (New York: Teachers College Press, 1999), ch. 2, and in Barry Allen Gold, "Punctuated Legitimacy: A Theory of Educational Change," *Teachers College Record* 101, no. 2 (1999): 192–219. The notion of the inevitability of technological changes is familiar. For example, in a speech entitled "Child Power: Keys to the New Learning of the Digital Century," Seymour Papert predicts that when the "cohort of young people who grew up with a computer from the beginning" have been in school for a while there will be an "irresistible pressure to change the structure and the content and the nature of schooling." http://www.connectedfamily.com/frame4/cf0413seymour/recent_essays/cf0413_cherry_2.html. Steven Gilbert, in "Making the Most of a Slow Revolution," makes a similar point for higher education since the 1970s. *Change*, March/April 1996, pp. 10–23.

36. James Beniger, *The Control Revolution: Technological and Economic Origins of the Information Society* (Cambridge: Harvard University Press, 1986), pp. 1–27.

37. Paul David, "The Dynamo and the Computer: A Historical Perspective on the Modern Productivity Paradox," *American Economic Review* 80 (May): 355–361.

38. Peter Drucker, "Beyond the Information Revolution," *Atlantic Monthly* 284, no. 4 (1999): 47–57.

39. Rogers, *Diffusion of Innovations*.

40. Based upon surveys, Henry Becker makes this argument which, in effect, says that increased access means increased use and increased use

will lead to more teachers adopting student-centered ("constuctivist" is Becker's word) teaching practices. See J. L. Ravitz, H. J. Becker, and Y-T Wong, "Constructivist-Compatible Beliefs and Practices among U.S. Teachers," Teaching, Learning, and Computing, 1998 National Survey, Report 4, Center for Research on Information technology and Organizations, University of California, Irvine, 1998.

41. Louis Uchitelle, "107 Months and Counting," *New York Times*, January 30, 2000, p. 1BU; Mary Walsh, "Productivity Takes Steep Jump," *Los Angeles Times*, November 13, 1999, p. C1. A less rosy view of the economic expansion is in Jeff Madrick, "How New Is the New Economy," *New York Review of Books*, September 23, 1999, pp. 42–50.

42. National Commission on Excellence in Education, *Nation at Risk* (Washington, DC: U.S. Government printing office, 1983).

43. See *Workforce 2000: Work and Workers for the Twenty-first Century* (Indianapolis: Hudson Institute, 1987); *Making America Work: Productive People, Productive Policies* (Washington, DC: National Governors' Association, 1988); The Secretary's Commission on Achieving Skills (SCAN), *What Work Requires of Schools* (Washington, DC: U.S. Department of Labor, 1991). For the pervasiveness of standards-based school reform, test scores, and accountability measures, see the special issue "Quality Counts: Rewarding Results, Punishing Failure," *Education Week*, January 11, 1999.

44. "Technology Counts," *Education Week*, November 10, 1997, p. 39.

45. Much of the following discussion on symbolism in organizations and applications to computers is drawn from the following sources: Henderson, *On Line and on Paper*, ch. 8; John Meyer and Brian Rowan, "Institutionalized Organizations: Formal Structure as Myth and Ceremony," in Walter Powell and Paul DiMaggio, eds., *The New Institutionalism in Organizational Analysis* (Chicago: University of Chicago Press, 1983), pp. 41–62; Jeffrey Pfeffer, "Management as Symbolic Action: The Creation and Maintenance of Organizational Paradigms," *Research in Organizational Behavior* 3, (1981): 1–52; Mark J. Zbaracki, "The Rhetoric and Reality of Total Quality Management," *Administrative Science Quarterly* 43, (1998): 602–636; James G. March and Johan P. Olsen, *Rediscovering Institutions: The Organizational Basis of Politics* (New York: Free Press, 1989), chs. 3, 5.

46. Henderson, *On Line and On Paper*, p. 189.

47. A similar phenomenon of rhetoric and reality and the importance of symbolic language can be seen in the Total Quality Management innovation that swept through the business sector in the 1980s. See Zbaracki, "The

Rhetoric and Reality of Total Quality Management." See also Thomas, *What Machines Can't Do*; Jeffrey Pfeffer and Gerald Salancik, *The External Control of Organizations* (New York: Harper and Row, 1979); John Meyer and Brian Rowan, "Institutionalized Organizations: Formal Structure as Myth and Ceremony," *American Journal of Sociology* 83, no. 2 (1977): 340–363; John Meyer, W. Richard Scott, and Terrence Deal, "Institutional and Technical Sources of Organizational Structure: Explaining the Structure of Educational Organizations," in John Meyer and W. Richard Scott, eds., *Organizational Environments: Ritual and Rationality* (Newbury Park, CA: Sage Publications, 1992), pp. 45–70.

Context as a factor in explaining teacher use of technologies has been investigated only occasionally. In one study of computer use in high schools in the mid-1980s, Janet Ward Schofield found that contextual factors had a profound influence on which teachers used computers for instruction, how the machines were used by students in classrooms, and the limits of technology use in the school itself. See *Computers and Classroom Culture* (New York: Cambridge University Press, 1995), pp. 190–228. Also see her "Computers and Classroom Social Processes: A Review of the Literature," *Social Science Computer Review* 15, no. 1 (1997): 27–39.

48. David K. Cohen's work on the interdependence between practice and policy embedded in the long history of schools as institutions pursues territory similar to this explanation. See, in particular, "Educational Technology, Policy, and Practice," *Educational Evaluation and Policy Analysis* 9, no. 2 (1987): 153–170.

49. See Julie Reuben, *The Making of the Modern University* (Chicago: University of Chicago Press, 1996); Laurence Veysey, *The Emergence of the American University* (Chicago: University of Chicago Press, 1965); and Roger Geiger, *To Advance Knowledge: The Growth of American Research Universities* (New York: Oxford University Press, 1986).

50. See Cuban, *How Scholars Trumped Teachers*, ch. 1.

51. For histories of the high school, see William Reese, *The Origins of the American High School* (New Haven: Yale University Press, 1995); Ed Krug, *The Shaping of the American High School*, vol. 1 (New York: Harper and Row, 1964); Robert Hampel, *The Last Little Citadel* (Boston: Houghton and Mifflin, 1986).

52. For the interaction between district decisions on class size, grouping, and allocation of funds shaping how teachers teach, see Rebecca Barr and Robert Dreeben, *How Schools Work* (Chicago: University of Chicago Press, 1983).

53. Barbara Beatty, *Preschool Education in America: The Culture of Young Children from the Colonial Period to the Present* (New Haven: Yale University Press, 1995).

54. Yong Zhao (Michigan State University) and Paul Conway (Cleveland State University) analyzed 15 state technology plans published in the mid-1990s. They found that the state plans viewed the computer as a "neutral cognitive tool." "What Is for Sale Today? And Analysis of State technology Plans," unpublished paper in author's possession. For an analysis of seeing technology as neutral see Langdon Winner, *Autonomous Technology* (Cambridge: MIT Press, 1977), pp. 198–205; Gene Rochlin, *Trapped in the Net: The Unanticipated Consequences of Computerization* (Princeton: University of Princeton Press, 1997), pp. 15–34.

55. Media reports on malfunctioning computer systems in buying stocks and hacker entry into high-security systems, plus a constant stream of ads for technical support, suggest that hardware and software flaws and failures are pervasive. Serious consequences may occur also. A month-long computer breakdown at the Pentagon's National Imagery and Mapping Agency, which collects and analyzes photographs from spy satellites, occurred in 1999. The agency provides high-resolution images, for example, of North Korea's nuclear weapons sites, Chinese naval deployment, and Iraq's rebuilding of chemical weapons plants. Intelligence officials needed the photos for analyses, which they sent directly to the President and his national security advisers. High costs for the new technology and malfunctioning computers stopped the flow of photographs for well over a month. James Risen, "Computer Ills Meant U.S. Couldn't Read Its Spy Photographs," *New York Times,* April 12, 2000, pp. 1, A20.

56. Donald Norman, *The Invisible Computer* (Cambridge: MIT Press, 1999), p. 81.

57. Ibid., pp. 80–81. Also see James Gorman, "Unlikely Warrior Leads the Charge for Simpler PC," *New York Times,* June 24, 1997, pp. B9, B13.

58. Ronald J. Abate, "Teaching Practices and the Design of Professional Development Activities," paper presented at the Society for Information Technology and Teacher Education conference in San Diego, CA, February 2000.

59. That district decisions affect the social organization of the school has been one element in this explanation. But the influence of district decisions on schools is far from monolithic. Schools vary in how each one organizes itself, creates norms that guide teachers about what is good and poor teaching, and creates a culture of learning. See Susan Rosenholtz,

Teachers' Workplace: The Social Organization of Schools (New York: Longman, 1989).

60. David Cohen, "Educational Technology and School Organization," in Raymond Nickerson and Philip Zodhiates, eds., *Technology in Education: Looking toward 2020* (Hillsdale, NJ: Erlbaum, 1990), pp. 231–264.; Michael Fullan, *The New Meaning of Educational Change* (New York: Teachers College Press, 1991); Susan Moore Johnson, *Teachers at Work* (New York: Basic Books, 1990); Milbrey McLaughlin, "What Matters Most in Teachers Workplace Context?" in M. McLaughlin and J. Little, eds., *Teachers Work* (New York: Teachers College Press, 1993), pp. 79–103; Michael Huberman, "The Model of the Independent Artisan in Teachers' Professional Relations," in *Teachers Work*, pp. 11–50.

61. These questions have been called the "practicality ethic" common to teachers. I have amended the wording of some questions and added others drawn from teacher interviews. The idea comes from Walter Doyle and Gerald Ponder, "The Practicality Ethic in Teacher Decision," *Interchange* 8 (1977–1978): 1–12. Rogers uses the concept of compatibility to make a similar point in *Diffusion of Innovations*, pp. 223–226. Also see Rudolph van den Berg and Anje Ros, "The Permanent Importance of the Subjective Reality of Teachers during Educational Innovation," *American Educational Research Journal* 36, no. 4 (1999): 879–906.

62. One exception is a study by Stephen Barley, "Technology as an Occasion for Structuring: Evidence from Observations of CT Scanners and the Social Order of Radiology Departments," *Administrative Science Quarterly* 31 (1986): 78–108. Barley investigated how the same technology—a CT Scanner—was installed in two hospitals and how the organizational structures and interactions among radiologists and technicians caused two very different structures to emerge in these hospitals. The mutual adaptations that occurred displays nicely that a new technology does not determine what occurs in organizations but simply is one of many elements that influence patterns of organizational action. Charles Perrow, "The Organizational Context of Human Factors Engineering," *Administrative Science Quarterly* 28, no. 4 (1983): 521–541. Also see Henderson and Thomas case studies.

63. Steve Farkas and Jean Johnson, "Given the Circumstances: Teachers Talk about Public Education Today" (New York: Public Agenda, 1996), p. 25; Dan Lortie, *Schoolteacher* (Chicago: University of Chicago Press, 1975).

64. Lortie, *Schoolteacher,* pp. 101–109, 187–200.

65. Richard Prawat, *Changing Schools by Changing Teachers' Beliefs*

about *Teaching and Learning* (East Lansing: Michigan State University, Center for the Learning and Teaching of Elementary Subjects, 1990); James Calderhead, "Teachers: Beliefs and Knowledge," in David Berliner and Robert Calfee, eds., *Handbook of Educational Psychology* (New York: Macmillan, 1996), pp. 709–725; Ravitz, Becker, and Wong, "Constructivist-Compatible Beliefs and Practices among U.S. Teachers."

66. A Principal Scientist at BNN Corporation and Professor of Education at Northwestern University, Allan Collins, described his experiences teaching physical sciences in 1990 to fifth- and sixth-grade classes for 20 sessions, each lasting about two hours, in a Cambridge, Massachusetts, elementary school. With 10 MacIIs, a network, a library of books, and various software (*Physics Explorer* and *Table Top*), Collins organized the classes around big questions such as: why the moon appears to follow you around? How the earth formed? Why all the planets do not fall into the sun? Students wrote up answers to the questions and put them into hypercard stacks for others to read. "One of the things I learned from the experience," Collins wrote, "was how awkwardly current computer technology fits into schools." He meant how little available space there was in the classroom for the machines, cables, and accessories. After moving the machines into a lab, he said that "this meant the class had to move from the classroom whenever they wanted to work on their projects, which took time and caused confusion." After his experience in an elementary school, he concluded: "The structures and conception of school that evolved in the last century is quite incompatible with effective use of new technologies." "Whither Technology and Schools? Collected Thoughts on the Last and Next Quarter Centuries," in Charles Fisher and David Dwyer, eds., *Education and Technology: Reflections on Computing in Classrooms* (San Francisco: Jossey Bass Publishers, 1996), pp. 51–65.

67. Milbrey McLaughlin, "Implementation as Mutual Adaptation in Classroom Organization," in Dale Mann, ed., *Making Change Happen* (New York: Teachers College Press, 1978), pp. 19–31.; Dorothy Leonard-Barton, "Implementation as Mutual Adaptation of Technology and Organization, *Research Policy* 17 (1988): 251–267.

6. ARE COMPUTERS IN SCHOOLS WORTH THE INVESTMENT?

1. Scott Herhold, "Venturing to the Capital," *San Jose Mercury News,* January 22, 1997, p. 1.

2. U.S. Department of Commerce, "Falling Through the Net: Defining the Digital Divide," December 1998, (http://www.ntia.doc.gov/ntiahome/

fttn99/execsummary.html); Katie Hafner, "A Credibility Gap in the Digital Divide," *New York Times,* March 5, 2000, p. 4WK.

3. To underscore the point of divergent definitions, there now exist two sets of very different standards that invoke different versions of technological literacy because the groups issuing these standards each define technology differently. The International Society for Technology in Education published standards for instructional technology, particularly computers, in 1998. The International Technology Education Association published their standards for teaching about technology in 2000. Mary Ann Zehr, "National Standards on Tech Education Released," *Education Week,* April 12, 2000, (http://www.ntia.doc.gov/ntiahome/fttn99/execsummary.html). I am grateful to Henry Becker for pointing this out to me.

4. In a March 2000 survey of students ages 11–17, almost 80 percent had computers at home. Almost 60 percent used the computer at home daily. In very large percentages, they said that they use computers for school work, email, sports news, hobbies, games, and Web surfing. "NPR/Kaiser/Kennedy School Kids & Technology Survey," March 2, 2000, National Public Radio, Washington, DC, transcript available from Burrelle's, PO Box 7, Livingston, NJ 07039-0007. Alan Krueger, "How Computers Have Changed the Wage Structure: Evidence from Microdata, 1984–1989," *Quarterly Journal of Economics* 108, February 1993, pp. 34–60.

5. Heather Kirkpatrick and Larry Cuban, "Computers Make Kids Smarter—Right?" *Technos* 7, no. 2 (1998): 26–31; Thomas K. Landauer, *The Trouble with Computers: Usefulness, Usability, and Productivity* (Cambridge: MIT Press, 1995); W. Wayt Gibbs, "Taking Computers to Task," *Scientific American,* July 1997, pp. 82–89; Daniel E. Sichel, *The Computer Revolution: An Economic Perspective* (Washington, DC: Brookings Institution Press, 1997).

6. Henry Becker, "Findings from the Teaching, Learning, and Computing Survey: Is Larry Cuban Still Right?" Paper presented at Chief State School Officers Organization, Washington, DC, January 13, 2000.

7. My definition of success and failure is drawn from organizational effectiveness definitions, behavioral psychology, and recent application to medical practice. See *To Err Is Human: Building a Safer Health System* (Washington, DC: National Academy Press, 1999), p. 28. The definitions of success and failure are deeply rational in the weight placed on explicit goals and measurable indicators of whether the goals have been wholly or partially achieved.

8. Jason Ravitz, Henry Becker, and YanTien Wong, "Schools of the Future," Special Report, *Business Week Online*, September 25, 2000, http://www.businessweek.com/2000/00_39/b3700116.htm.

9. For an elaboration of an ecological view of technologies, see Ruth S. Cowan, "The Consumption Junction: A Proposal for Research Strategies in the Sociology of Technology," in W. Bijker, T. Hughes, and T. Pinch, eds., *The Social Construction of Technological Systems* (Cambridge: MIT Press, 1987), pp. 261–280; Thomas Davenport, *Information Ecology: Mastering the Information and Knowledge Environment* (New York: Oxford University Press, 1997). One curriculum project designed by professors at Vanderbilt University for use in schools and classrooms created imaginative software for fifth graders that would strengthen their mathematical thinking and bridge subject matter in science and social studies. Called the Jasper Project, the "Cognition and Technology Group" at Vanderbilt University worked with hundreds of teachers and thousands of students in Nashville, Tennessee, and elsewhere in using 12 videodiscs based on adventures of Jasper Woodbury. The staff learned over the seven years of the handsomely funded project several "major lessons." One involved "a much deeper appreciation of the importance of sociocultural contexts and their effects on learning." This innocuous phrasing masked the deep political conflicts that arose in some districts during the project that brought their work to a standstill. The Cognition and Technology Group at Vanderbilt, *The Jasper Project: Lessons in Curriculum, Instruction, Assessment, and Professional Development* (Hillsdale, NJ: Erlbaum, 1997), p. 157.

10. Jane David, *Results in Education: State Actions to Restructure Schools* (Washington, DC: National Governors Association, 1990); Fred Newmann, Bruce King, and Mark Rigdon, "School Accountability: Implications from Restructuring Schools," *Harvard Educational Review* 67 (1997): 41–74; Richard Elmore, Penelope Peterson, and Sarah McCarthy, *Restructuring in the Classroom: Teaching, Learning, and School Organization* (San Francisco: Jossey-Bass, 1996).

11. Ernest Boyer, *Scholarship Reconsidered: Priorities of the Professoriate* (Princeton: Carnegie Foundation for the Advancement of Teaching, 1990); Boyer Commission Report, *Reinventing Undergraduate Education: A Blueprint for America's Research Universities* (Princeton: Carnegie Foundation for the Advancement of Teaching, 1998); Jodi Wilgoren, "A Revolution in Education Clicks into Place," *New York Times*, March 26, 2000, pp. 1, 27.

12. The overriding issue facing early childhood settings is not the inclusion of technologies in the curriculum; it is the unremitting pressure for academic preparation. See Irving Sigel, "Early Childhood Education: Developmental Enhancement Developmental Acceleration?" in Sharon Kagan and Edward Zigler, eds., *Early Schooling: The National Debate* (New Haven: Yale University Press, 1987), pp. 129–150.

13. Cowan, "The Consumption Junction."

14. For unexpected developments with professors in a university when technologies were introduced, see Sherry Turkle, "Paradoxical Reactions and Powerful Ideas: Educational Computing in a Department of Physics," in Mark Shields, ed., *Work and Technology in Higher Education* (Hillsdale, NJ: Erlbaum, 1995), pp. 37–63; and Paul Anderson, "Faculty and Student Observations of Their Computing Behavior," in Sara Kiesler and Lee Sproull, eds., *Computing and Change on Campus*, (New York: Cambridge University Press, 1987, pp. 90–100.

15. The director of the project, Harvey Pressman, drafted the proposal and secured the federal funds for the Berkeley Unified School District. He designed a project based on his work in Massachusetts with elementary schools using technology for the first time. I had known Pressman for many years, especially his work with special needs students. For the first four years of the project he hired me to be a "critical friend," that is, someone who would visit all of the sites, interview teachers, principals, district administrators, and project staff, observe what occurred in classrooms, and write a report for him summarizing what I saw and what improvements I would recommend. I did so between 1997 and 2000. At no point did Pressman ask me to shape the reports to his specifications or other audiences. I gave my descriptions, analysis, and recommendations freely and independently of his agenda, knowing full well that some things I said would sting the Director.

16. Berkeley Planning Associates, "Teacher Led Technology Challenge: Year Three Evaluation Report," November 1999.

17. I have drawn freely from the "Principles of Technorealism," a Website devoted to expanding "the fertile middle ground between techno-utopianism and neo-Luddism." See http://www/technorealism.org/overview.html

18. See James Coleman, "Social Capital in the Creation of Human Capital," in C. Winship and S. Rosen, eds., *Organizations and Institutions: Sociological and Economic Approaches to the Analysis of Social Structure,* suppl. to *American Journal of Sociology* 94 (1998): S95-S120. Social capi-

tal, like human and physical capital, can enhance individual lives and achieve societal goals, although, as Putnam and others point out, the networks of contacts and reciprocity within communities have a dark side as well. See Robert Putnam, *Bowling Alone* (New York: Simon and Schuster, 2000), pp. 18–19. His thesis and evidence about the decline in social capital since the 1970s has been challenged by critics who have questioned Putnam's reliance on membership in formal groups and his ignoring of emerging informal small groups including book clubs, card-playing groups, investment clubs, and new social movements. See Alejandro Portes, "Social Capital: Its Origins and Applications in Modern Sociology," *Annual Review of Sociology* 22 (1998), pp. 1–24; Robert Wurthnow, *Loose Connections: Joining Together in America's Fragmented Communities* (Cambridge: Harvard University Press, 1998); Everett Ladd, *The Ladd Report* (New York: Free Press, 1999).

19. Putnam, *Bowling Alone*, pp. 19, 287.
20. Ibid., pp. 404–406.
21. A statement from The Alliance for Childhood signed by educators, academics, and parents has called for a moratorium on purchasing computers for children below the age of 7, except for those with disabilities. I was one of the signers. The organization also issued a report, "Fool's Gold: A Critical Look at Computers in Childhood" (College Park, MD: Alliance for Childhood, 2000).
22. Francis Fitzgerald, *Way Out There in the Blue: Reagan, Star Wars, and the End of the Cold War* (New York: Simon and Schuster, 2000), pp. 19–41, 479–499. Also see Michael Oreskes, "Troubling the Waters of Nuclear Deterrence," *New York Times,* June 4, 2000, p. 3; Peter Boyer, "When Missiles Collide," *New Yorker,* September 11, 2000, pp. 42–48. Another example of powerful coalitions advocating technology even when tests reveal stro4ng reservations about their cost, safety, and overall worth is the Osprey, a U.S. Marine Corps aircraft that takes off and lands like a helicopter and flies like a plane. The Osprey carries twice as many troops much further and faster than helicopters can. In April 2000 an Osprey (costing $60 million) crashed, killing 19 Marines. There had been two previous crashes. The remaining 12 aircraft produced by the Boeing Company were grounded. On the basis of extensive testing and inspection of the experimental craft, top Pentagon officials in the Reagan, Bush, and Clinton administrations had recommended on numerous occasions canceling production on grounds of unreliability and cost. In each instance, Congress ignored the Pentagon recommendations

because lawmakers feared losing more than 125,000 manufacturing jobs in 40 states where Boeing and subcontractors had facilities. Tim Weiner, "For Military Plane in Crash, a History of Political Conflict," *New York Times,* April 11, 2000, p. A31; "Doubts about the High-Risk Osprey," *New York Times,* April 14, 2000, p. A30.

APPENDIX: RATIONALE FOR CHOICES OF SCHOOL LEVELS

1. Adapted from Ronald Anderson and Amy Ronnkvist, "The Presence of Computers in American Schools: Teaching, Learning, and Computing, the 1998 National Survey," Report #2, University of California, Irvine, and The University of Minnesota, Center for Research on Information Technology and Organizations, June 1999, p. 8.
2. Ibid., p. 12
3. Ibid., pp. 8–9, 21.
4. U.S. Department of Education, National Center for Educational Statistics, "Teachers' Tools for the 21st Century: A Report on Teacher Use of Technology," September 2000, NCES 2000–102, pp. 67–69.
5. Ibid.
6. U.S. Department of Commerce, Bureau of the Census, *Current Population Survey, 1993 and 1997,* unpublished data, table 428, p. 484.
7. See Hersholt Waxman and Shwu-Yong Huang, "Classroom Instruction Differences by Level of Technology Use in Middle School Mathematics," *Journal of Educational Computing Research* 14, no. 2 (1996): 157–169; Debra Mathinos and Arthur Woodward, "Instructional Computing in an Elementary School: The Rhetoric and Reality of an Innovation," *Journal of Curriculum Studies* 20, no. 5 (1988): 465–473; Hugh Mehan, "Microcomputers in Classrooms: Educational Technology or Social Practice," *Anthropology and Education Quarterly* 20 (1989): 4–22; Judith Sandholtz, Cathy Ringstaff, and David Dwyer, *Teachers and Technology* (New York: Teachers College Press, 1997). One study done of high school teachers and students using computers is Janet W. Schofield, *Computers and Classroom Culture* (New York: Cambridge University Press, 1995).

For research that has investigated the gaps between teachers' self-reports of their practice and what researchers observed of the teachers in their classrooms, see Laurence Antil, Joseph Jenkins, Susan Wayne, and Patricia Vadasy, "Cooperative Learning: Prevalence, Conceptualizations, and the Relation between Research and Practice," *American*

Educational Research Journal 35, no. 3 (1998): 419–454; James Spillane and John Zeuli, "Reform and Teaching: Exploring Patterns of Practice in the Context of National and State Mathematics Reforms," *Educational Evaluation and Policy Analysis* 21, no. 1 (1999): 1–27; Daniel Mayer, "Measuring Instructional Practice: Can Policymakers Trust Survey Data?" *Educational Evaluation and Policy Analysis* 21, no. 1 (1999): 29–45.

ACKNOWLEDGMENTS

This book began on a bike ride with David Tyack in the mid-1990s. While climbing hills, sweating and puffing professors talk a lot to ease the work of cranking those pedals. David, a dear friend and colleague with whom I had team-taught for many years and coauthored a book, thought it would be worthwhile to revisit the history and policy of technology in schools, a subject I had written about a decade earlier. I was not so sure; but after that ride and subsequent ones, the idea intrigued me.

After rereading my *Teachers and Machines: The Classroom Uses of Technology since 1920* and considering the literature on new technologies in schools, I became convinced that few researchers know about past uses of technological innovations in schools, and even fewer researchers sit in classrooms, interview teachers and students, and investigate how new technologies are actually used in schools. In fact, most data on school and classroom use of new machines comes from the self-reports of practitioners, professors, technology coordinators, and superintendents. While self-reports are useful in filling in the picture, they are only one of several sources of evidence we need for an accurate view of what actually happens in classrooms. So I decided to do a qualitative study that would combine a history of school technologies, surveys, and interviews with statistical data collected at the school site and direct observation of classroom practices.

Over the last four years many people have given generously of their time to help me conduct this study. Foremost, I am indebted to the principals, teachers, and students who graciously permitted us to enter their school lives and document their work. Unfortunately, because of promised confidentiality, I cannot name these practitioners and students, but anonymity does not lessen the essential contributions they have made to this project. I am most grateful to all of them.

And I am delighted to be able to acknowledge publicly those foundations, graduate students, colleagues, and others who have made this book possible. For providing funds to hire three graduate students over several years to research the published literature I thank the Center for Ecoliteracy (in collaboration with Learning in the Real World). The Spencer Foundation made funds available for two doctoral students to investigate Bay Area high schools. Finally, in 1999–2000, the Center for Advanced Study in the Behavioral Sciences provided uninterrupted time, superb colleagues, helpful staff, and volleyball companions, without whom this book might not have been written.

Avis Austin, Heather Kirkpatrick, Huey Ru Lin, Craig Peck, and Lawrence Tovar gave unstintingly of their talents and time as graduate students to work with me between 1997 and 2000. I am deeply appreciative of their critical contributions to this study and to the book.

Many readers of the manuscript offered comments and queries that helped me improve the final draft. For their generous advice and support I wish to acknowledge Sondra Cuban, Elisabeth Hansot, Linda Labbo, Gary Lichtenstein, Kathleen Much, Stan Pesick, Buddy Peshkin, Harvey Pressman, David Tyack, and Decker Walker. Henry Becker and an anonymous reviewer read the manuscript for Harvard University Press and provided excellent critiques and suggestions for improving the manuscript. Joel Merenstein offered resources on evidence-based medicine that were invaluable to me.

Finally, I thank my editor, Elizabeth Knoll, whose enthusiasm for the book and thoughtful responses encouraged me to complete the book far sooner than I would have.

Larry Cuban
Stanford University
February 2001

INDEX

Abecedarian project, 46
America, 4; Civil War and, 8–9; Cold War and, 9–10; gold fever and, 21–22; early transportation and, 22–23; historical educational views of, 40–45; control revolutions and, 153; Star Wars campaign and, 192–193
Apple Computer, 104, 112, 165
Astor, Randy, 79

Badillo, Anna, 26–27
Baldwin preschool, 50–51, 53, 55
Bell Kindergarten, 50–51, 53, 55
Beniger, James, 152–153
Benjamin co-op preschool, 36–39, 50–51, 55
Bloom, Benjamin, 41
Boyd, Stephen, 125–126
Brain development: early exposure to computers and, 60–67; synapse formation, 62; brainstorming, 116. *See also* Education
Bruno, Ed, 27, 29
Bryce, James, 24
Bush, George, 44, 156, 193

California schools, 31, 33–35; Proposition 13 and, 13, 30, 32, 74; enigma of, 21–22; immigrants and, 22–23; history of, 22–24; workaholism of, 27–30; Benjamin preschool and, 36–39, 50–

51, 55; George Elementary School and, 47; frequency of computer use and, 58–67, 71–73; Las Montañas High School and, 73–77, 81–82, 84–85, 89–93, 161–162; Flatland High School and, 78–93. *See also* Silicon Valley
Casper, Gerhard, 110, 116, 124
Center for Educational Research at Stanford (CERAS), 100–101
Chambers, John, 102
Clements, Douglas, 61–64
Clinton, Bill, 15–18, 156, 193
Cohen, David, 95
Commission on Technology in Teaching and Learning (CTTL), 124
Commission on Undergraduate Education (CUE), 115
Computer-Aided-Design (CAD), 80, 142, 144
Computers, 11; school reform and, 12–20; cost of, 17–18, 176–197; frequency and use of, 17–18, 58–67, 71–73; Benjamin preschool and, 36–39, 50–51, 55; California study and, 49–58; in home, 54–56, 84–85; teachers' attitude and, 56–58; brain development and, 60–61; creative integration of, 68–71; Las Montañas High School and, 73–77, 81–82, 84–85, 89–93, 161–162; Flatland High School and, 78–93; minimal effect of, 93–98; Stanford Univer-

Computers *(continued)*
sity and, 99–130; university spending and, 104–107; unexpected consequences of, 131–175; increased communication and, 133; academic achievement and, 133–134; as status symbols, 158–159. *See also* Silicon Valley

Corporations, 4, 11; school reform and, 7; technology and, 12–20; Silicon Valley and, 24–30; work ethics and, 27–29; California schools and, 31; Honig and, 32; Las Montañas and, 75–76; universities and, 103–104; hierarchical challenges of, 141–146; skunk-works strategy and, 143–144; teaching contexts and, 158; software design and, 165

David, Paul, 153
Davis, Gray, 32
Desegregation, 32
Diaz, Hector, 85–89
Didion, Joan, 21
Digital High School grants, 33, 76–77
Doerr, John, 176

Eastin, Delaine, 33
Ecker, Joseph, 102
Economics, 4; school reform and, 7; history and, 8–10; computer costs and, 17–18; transportation and, 22–24; Silicon Valley and, 24–33; Great Depression, 40–41; preschool and, 43–44; parents and, 66; Stanford and, 111–113; control revolutions and, 152–153; computer investment value and, 176–197; social capital and, 190–197
Education: bashing of, 1; history of, 2–10; homeschooling and, 3; power of, 4; as economy's servant, 8; downsizing and, 10–11; technology and, 12–20; real life and, 14–15; student-centered teaching,

14–15, 96, 134; employment and, 15–16; problem-based, 117; project-based, 117; Master Plan and, 31; Benjamin preschool and, 36–39; academic preparedness and, 39–45; history and, 40–45; Head Start and, 42–44; preschool evaluation and, 45–49; California study and, 49–58; early exposure to computers and, 60–67; creative integration and, 68–71; visual presentations and, 68–71; Las Montañas High School and, 73–77, 81–82, 84–85, 89–93, 161–162; Flatland High School and, 78–93; technology's minimal effect, 93–98; LGI and, 99–101; SCRDT and, 99–100; distance, 103; lectures and, 105–106, 115–121, 125; research and, 107–110; Stanford and, 107–130; Socratic method, 116; unexpected consequences and, 131–175; low-tech approach and, 137–138, 163–164; contexts of, 156–159; learning atmosphere and, 162–164; constrained choice and, 167–170; keyboarding and, 177; future goals for, 180–184, 193; TLTC and, 184–188; social capital and, 190–197
Educational Summit, 15–16
Elkind, David, 61
Email, 29, 56, 127; Flatland High School and, 83; professors and, 105
Employment, 11, 15–16, 160–161; Flatland High School and, 80–81; computer literacy and, 178
Engineers, 141–146
Englemann-Bereiter preschool, 46
Evidence-Based Medicine (EBM), 147–150

Faculty Author Development (FAD) program, 112, 124, 126
Flatland High School, 78–81; technological access and, 82–84; home computer